ANYBODY CAN BE COOL

...But Awesome Takes Practice

LORRAINE PETERSON

BETHANY HOUSE PUBLISHERS

MINNEAPOLIS, MINNESOTA 55438
A Division of Bethany Fellowship, Inc.

Published by Bethany House Publishers
A Division of Bethany Fellowship, Inc.
6820 Auto Club Road, Minneapolis, Minnesota 55438

Printed in the United States of America

Library of Congress Cataloging-in-Publication Data

Peterson, Lorraine.
  Anybody can be cool—but awesome takes practice.

(Devotionals for teens)
  1. Teenagers—Prayer-books and devotions—English.
I. Title.
BV4850.P44   1988   242'.63   88-19454
ISBN 1-55661-040-8

About the Author

LORRAINE PETERSON was born in Red Wing, Minnesota, grew up on a farm near Ellsworth, Wisconsin, and now resides in Guadalajara, Mexico. She received her B.A. (in history) from North Park College in Chicago, and has taken summer courses from the University of Minnesota and the University of Mexico in Mexico City.

Lorraine has taught high school and junior high. She has been an advisor to nondenominational Christian clubs in Minneapolis public schools and has taught teenage Bible studies. She has written several bestselling devotional books for teens:

If God Loves Me, Why Can't I Get My Locker Open?
Falling Off Cloud Nine and Other High Places
Why Isn't God Giving Cash Prizes?
Real Characters in the Making
Dying of Embarrassment & Living to Tell About It
Anybody Can Be Cool, But Awesome Takes Practice
If the Devil Made You Do It, You Blew It!
Radical Advice From the Ultimate Wise Guy
If You Really Trust Me, Why Can't I Stay Out Later?

Preface

I'd listened to a lot of Bible teachings given by John Larson and had always found them helpful. However, his series of talks on Scripture meditation proved to be of lasting value in my life, giving me the framework for enjoying the benefits of daily internalizing more of God's Word. John originated most of the ideas for the card at the end of each devotional. I decided that I'd put John's exhortation into practice. I began taking memory verse cards with me any time I thought I'd have an extra minute to think—jogging, waiting for a friend, walking to the store, even listening to the music on the telephone and hearing the familiar "calls are being taken in the order received. Please do not hang up." Sometimes I just sit down in the middle of cleaning the closet or planning the week's activities to repeat a Bible verse over and over, putting my name in it and applying it to my situation. When I attended Bill Gothard's Basic Youth Conflict's seminar again, he, too, emphasized Scripture meditation. The most helpful concept he added to what I had already learned was: "Always fall asleep meditating on Scripture." The decision I made to internalize Scripture (not just read it once or twice a day) and to take practical steps to "meditate on it day and night" have brought me closer to Jesus and have helped me conquer thoughts that used to torment me. I don't intend to ever stop carrying around my memory verse cards or selecting a passage of God's Word each night to "dream with." Because of the blessing I've received from Scripture meditation, I want to share this "secret" with my teenage audience. At the same time, I was learning more about who I am in Christ. I began to see that I'd accepted many lies about myself which needed to be replaced with God's truth. The Bible really says that I'm a new creature in Christ Jesus. In Him, I am strong, I am loved, and I'm a winner—more than conqueror in fact. I am the light of the world. Jesus said so. I wanted to combine these two themes into a book for teenagers: an adventure in letting Scripture remake your self-image. I would like to thank the people whose contributions to my life have made the writing of this book possible. Reading *Telling Yourself the Truth* by William Backus and Marie Chapian; *Birthright* by David Needham; and *Building Your Self-Image* by Josh McDowell provided me with needed background material. I want to express my appreciation to my family for their support and help. My roommate, Juanita, has prayed for this book and has been very kind to its author. Not only did God use John Larson to inspire the basic format of this book, but he and his wife, Linda, have been an encouragement to me. A special thanks goes to Michael O'Connor for proofreading this manuscript and sharing his deep insights into Scripture, which have not only influenced my writing, but also my life.

Lorraine Peterson

Contents

8

Introduction

Instead of attending the Bible studies, participating in organized recreation, going swimming, and showing up at the evening services, Sarah[1], a tenth grader, confined herself to her cabin. Because of an allergic reaction, her face was puffy and red. As her counselor, I tried to coax her to join in with the rest. But when I realized how deep her self-consciousness and insecurity was, I came back to the cabin every afternoon to take her for a walk on the overgrown path that led to the dump—the only place where no one would see us!

I was on lunchroom duty in a large inner city high school. Suddenly two hundred students rushed toward one table. Trying to form a plan in my mind for putting down the revolution, I hastened to investigate. I saw Rusty[2] reach into his pocket and pull out a plastic bag containing some water and a wriggling gold fish. He swallowed it alive in front of an admiring audience, reached out his hand for the five dollar bill his friend had promised for successful execution of this feat, and sat down to eat corndogs and macaroni salad with the air of a hero.

Self-consciousness, feelings of inferiority, the compulsion to show off, and the need to gain peer approval

---

[1]Name has been changed.
[2]Name has been changed.

regardless of the consequences are realities of the teen scene. Even Christians have tremendous problems and are often unable to view themselves as God sees them. The purpose of this book is to answer the often-asked question, "Who am I?" from a totally scriptural point of view. "The truest thing about ourselves is what the Bible says."[3]

After you invite Jesus to live His life within you, the Bible explains the truth about the new you. As you discover what God says about you and incorporate these scriptures into your self-image, you become free to express your true personality—a unique and beautifully designed mirror to reflect Jesus to the world.

In spite of the many books that have been written about self-image and self-improvement, a basic principle of the Bible has often been ignored: "For our struggle is not against flesh and blood, but against the rulers, against authorities, against the powers of this dark world and against the spiritual forces of evil in the heavenly realms" (Eph. 6:12). Although the spirit of the person who really knows Jesus has the special protection of the Holy Spirit, "with whom you were sealed for the day of redemption" (Eph. 4:30), the devil and his demons often attack the minds and emotions of Christians.

Throughout the Scriptures, we see Satan in the role of accuser. He accused Job of following God just because everything was going well for him. In Zech. 3:1 we find a description of a vision in which Satan is standing near Joshua the high priest accusing. Rev. 12:10 presents the devil as "the accuser of our brothers, who accuses them before our God day and night."

It is only God's truth that can refute the accusations of the devil and free the person to see himself or herself from God's point of view. "Once you were alienated from God and were enemies in your minds because of your evil behavior. But now he has reconciled you by Christ's physical body through death to present you holy in his sight,

---

[3]Josh McDowell, *Building Your Self-Image* (Wheaton, Ill.: Tyndale House Publishers, 1986), p. 129.

without blemish *and free from accusation—if you continue in your faith, established and firm* not moved from the hope held out in the gospel" (Col. 1:21–23).

Stating that we must learn to live out God's definition of our true identity instead of Satan's does not negate human will or the uniqueness of personality. Prov. 16:1 tells us: "To man belong the plans of the heart"—a capacity for creative thinking. God did not make robots. However, the human mind is a battlefield in which the devil uses his lies to try to capture God's special creations for himself. In order to live victoriously, one must learn to accept outside input only from God.

But tuning in to Lucifer's Lying Network isn't the only reason for confusion and failure. Many problems are caused by willful disobedience to God's will. For example, the person who chooses sex before marriage must live with the consequences of that action. Only setting aside all self-justification and truly repenting will get the person back on track. Lack of self-discipline, not allowing our spirits to receive instruction from God in order to tell our bodies what to do, is another problem. It works like this: If you don't tell your body to go to bed at a decent hour on Saturday night in order to be alert and receptive during Sunday school and church, you'll be a malnourished Christian. And you really can't blame the devil. *You* did not control your body and help it to do God's will.

Disobeying God and lack of self-discipline are serious impediments to the expression of your true identity in Christ. In this book, however, I want to show how you can deal scripturally with thoughts and accusations from the devil that are designed to ruin your Christian self-image. You should expect the devil to attack your mind and emotions. When tragedy strikes, he'll try to keep you from thinking: "In all things God works for the good of those who love him" and tell you, "Now you'll have to face the rest of your life with an emotional handicap." If your friend lets you down, Satan will organize a special attack force of demons to keep you from opening your Bible and reading, "Be kind and compassionate to one another, forgiving each other, just as in Christ God forgave you" (Eph. 4:32). Instead, he'll try to turn your feelings of rejection against you by offering either bitterness or a "I'm-not-good-enough-for-anyone-to-love" syndrome. You need to adopt a winning strategy to overcome the one who "prowls around like a roaring lion looking for someone to devour," the enemy who knows that marring your self-image is one of his best methods of attack.

An example can best illustrate my point. You've been attending Student Venture Tuesday night meetings regularly, have accepted Christ, and have decided to do everything possible to win your world for Christ. But last Tuesday night was the only time you could see your aunt and uncle who had flown in from another state, and your parents insisted that you stay home. On Saturday when you show up at Bill's house for the previously announced discipleship training class, his mother informs you that the whole club has gone out-of-town for a weekend ski trip. You know that the staff workers haven't bothered to try to call because your mom left no phone messages. Although Judy's locker is in the same row as yours, she never mentioned anything. Tom could have said something to you in English class, but he didn't.

Taking advantage of your disappointment and hurt feelings, the devil stages a full-scale, lonely, left-out loser attack: "The kids who act like such good Christians are all hypocrites. Besides, they don't really accept you. If you weren't such a nerd, everybody would have invited you. Don't ever go back again. Christianity sounds nice, but it will never help you conquer your complexes."

Once Satan attacks, the ball is in your court. Are you going to agree with the devil and become depressed and bitter? Are you going to turn your back on God because of the failure of other Christians?

Or you could try playing martyr: "I'm following God so closely that I don't need any other people. The reason they didn't invite me on the ski weekend is that I'm too spiritual for them and my presence makes them feel uncomfortable. I'll just have to be a shining example so they feel guilty for treating me as they do." Although the spiritual-giant speal has a nice religious ring to it, it's still the devil's dissertation.

BUT THERE IS AN ALTERNATIVE. It's replacing the devil's lies with God's truth. Let God's Word form your thoughts: "Love covers over a multitude of sins" (1 Pet. 4:8). You can decide to love and forgive regardless of the reason you were not invited. You can also meditate on Scripture: "Not that I have already . . . been made perfect, but I press on to take hold of that for which Christ Jesus took hold of me . . . forgetting what is behind and straining toward what is ahead, I press on toward the goal to win the prize for which God has called me heavenward" (Phil. 3:12–14). You can face the possibility of needing to remodel something in your personality without falling apart. Remember that you are a new creature in Christ and that God will show you how to peel off those undesirable traits which form a hard shell around your true personality in Jesus. You can trust God to use the whole experience for your benefit.

Jesus set the example. Instead of concentrating on how hungry He was and how easy it would be to turn stones into bread, He thought: "I will live by every word that comes from the mouth of God—not my every idea that comes out when the devil opens his big trap." Jesus didn't dwell on how neat it would be to create a superman sensation by floating down from the temple to preach to a cheering crowd. His mind was on: "Do not put the Lord your God to the test." He never considered worshiping the devil to take over all the world's kingdoms. He filled His thoughts with "Worship the Lord your God and serve him only."

I'd like to quote from the explanation of the role of Scripture in character building given by Marilyn Hickey to a discouraged reader:

> The Bible has a lot to say about controlling an "uncontrollable" mind. God has strongly stated that we are to pull down strongholds, cast down imaginations, and bring every thought into the obedience of Christ (2 Cor. 10:4–5).

Here's some advice when the devil tries to get you to be down on yourself: Ask the Holy Spirit to reveal to you where or when that first thought came in. Then speak aloud to that thought commanding it to come under obedience to the mind of Christ. Claim the mind of Christ and perhaps speak another verse the Lord may reveal to you. You are on your way to destroying an evil stronghold and replacing it with the stronghold of God's word.

What will happen? You will begin to think according to the mind of Christ, the Holy Spirit within you, and imaginations will crumble. If mental harassment still occurs, start memorizing Scripture! It's a tremendous way to cleanse your mind. It's the "washing of the water of the word." And if you meditate on Scripture, you'll find that the devil won't dare torment.[4]

Someone has wisely stated: "You are what you think about all day long." We often express the same idea with less finesse: "Garbage in. Garbage out." So the only completely safe way to alter your personality is to meditate on Scripture.

In order to let God transform your thinking, two things are necessary: (1) Believing that the Bible is literally true and will work—being willing to throw out all other theories and systems of knowledge that do not COMPLETELY conform to God's Word. (2) Developing a system of putting so much of God's Word into your heart and mind that you'll be able to recognize the devil's lies and refute them immediately.

Going into detail, the first step involves taking Scripture at face value. Jesus said: "Apart from me you can do nothing"—period. We have a tendency to modify it, to revise it, and even to correct it until it reads: "People can do great things with a little help from Jesus." We accept nearly every trend in modern thinking with a spoonful of Christianity added. We quote Prov. 3:5–7, but we do not live by it. "Trust in the Lord with all your heart and *lean not on your own understanding*; in *all* your ways ac-

[4]Marilyn Hickey, "First Aid for Backsliding," *Charisma and Christian Life* (March 1988), p. 12.

knowledge him, and he will make your paths straight. (You mean mine are crooked?) *Do not be wise in your own eyes,* fear the Lord and shun evil." If we took God's Word seriously, we would not assume that "psychological laws" (and these so-called "psychological laws" differ greatly, depending on what book you read and what theory you accept) *must* be used to fill in the gaps that Scripture does not cover. We'd remember that Jesus said, "When he, the Spirit of truth, comes, he will guide you into all truth" (John 16:13). Prayerfully seeking God's answers for the things we do not understand would be a lot healthier than swallowing the prescription the world is currently dishing out.

After deciding that God's Word has more power than any human system, it is necessary to get enough of it into your mind and spirit so that you can successfully fight wrong ideas and mental attacks of Satan. Because he felt such a strong presence of evil, Martin Luther once threw an ink bottle at the devil. Using Scripture as your weapon, however, will not only be more effective; it will save the wallpaper in your room. How do you use the "sword of the Spirit," which is the Word of God? You need to make the Bible part of you by learning to meditate on it and to fill your thoughts with it.

The Bible actually promises success to those who meditate on God's Word. "Do not let this Book of the Law depart from your mouth; meditate on it day and night, so that you may be careful to do everything written in it. Then you will be prosperous and successful" (Josh. 1:8). "But his delight is in the law of the Lord, and on his law he meditates day and night. He is like a tree planted by streams of water, which yields its fruit in season and whose leaf does not wither. Whatever he does prospers" (Ps. 1:2–3).

The Apostle Paul proclaims that renewing your mind will transform your life. So it's not surprising that this fact has been affirmed by scientific investigation. Dr. Paul Meier did an extensive research study which proved that "students who had practiced almost daily Scripture meditation for *three years or longer* came out statistically significantly healthier and happier than students who did not meditate on Scripture daily."[5] Dr. Meier concludes: "Daily meditation on Scripture (with personal application) is the most effective means of obtaining personal joy, peace, and emotional maturity."[6]

[5]Paul Meier, M.D., *Meditating for Success* (Grand Rapids, Mich.: Baker House, 1985), p. 22.
[6]Ibid., p. 24.

STOP!

If you haven't invited Jesus to live within you so that the supernatural power of His Spirit is available to you, nothing written in this book will work for you. BUT YOU CAN DECIDE TO GIVE YOUR LIFE TO JESUS RIGHT NOW. HERE'S HOW.

First, realize that God is great and powerful and perfect—so awesome that you (and every other human) are sinful, weak, and helpless when it comes to pleasing Him and living up to His standards. There are no good works or systems of rituals that will make you right with God. The Bible says: "For all have sinned and fall short of the glory of God" (Rom. 3:23). Although God created us with many talents and abilities, we're all like cars without motors—unable to complete the real purpose for which we were born: preparing ourselves for heaven. Despite the fact that some people are deluxe models, the new clean heart (the motor so to speak) must come from outside ourselves. We are unable to produce pure hearts by human processes.

Second, remember the good news is that God loves you exactly as you are and He sent Jesus to die on the cross to erase your sin. He has the power to remake you. The Bible refers to this process as being "born again."

Third, you don't become a real Christian by osmosis. The Bible explains: "Yet to all who *received* him, to those who believed in his name, he gave the right to become children of God" (John 1:12). What does it really mean to receive Christ? First of all, you must stop trusting in your own ability to be good and confide completely in Jesus. Then it's necessary to totally repent of your sin—not just feel sorry about the mess you got yourself into because of your disobedience. Learn to hate sin and turn from it. You need to give yourself to Jesus without reservations and invite Him to come in and remodel your life. Let Jesus be your boss and obey His orders. You must determine to follow what the Bible says even if nobody else does and even when you could think of ten good reasons for doing it your way!

If you want to surrender your life to Jesus, here is a model prayer: "Dear Jesus, I'm inviting you to come into my life right now and affirming that you have the right to tell me what to do. I ask you to forgive my sin and give me the power to stop doing wrong things. I will obey you and follow you. Thank you for coming into my life according to your promise."

PART 1

In Jesus I Am the Person God Created Me to Be

So that the name of our Lord Jesus may be glorified in you and you in him, according to the grace of our God and the Lord Jesus Christ.

2 Thessalonians 1:12

The Exasperating Experiment

Tiffany glanced at herself in the mirror one last time. She had spent an hour putting on her makeup and combing her hair just right. Her dress was the most expensive she had ever worn. Although she wished she could instantly lose fifteen pounds and that her nose were shorter, she had done the very best she could to make herself attractive. She had been invited to Jewell's party, the equivalent of instant membership in Central High's VIP club. It was her chance to shake off the "boring and born-again" label. Besides, Todd, the strikingly handsome captain of the basketball team, was sure to be there, and Tiffany wanted to prove to him that she had more on the ball than his present girlfriend Sue.

Ignoring the still small voice warning her against hypocrisy, jealousy, and compromise, she flitted out the door, starring in her own version of "The Perfect Saturday Night." By the time she arrived, she had cast herself into the role of a vivacious but slightly sophisticated "go-along-with-the-crowd" celebrity. She pretended not to notice that Jewell's parents weren't home and accepted the drinks she was offered. She laughed at the fast-lane jokes and joined in putting down the "Kool-Aid Kids"—those who would need a lot of assistance if they were ever to be as cool as the in-crowd. Having had no acquaintance with alcoholic beverages, Tiffany didn't realize their effect. Downing one drink after another as if it were Coca-Cola, she first became dizzy and then sick to her stomach. The reflection she saw in the bathroom mirror bore no resemblance to the pretty girl who had left the house three hours before. Nor did the walls protect her from cruel laughter and jokes at her expense. Her eyes filled with tears, but she didn't have the courage to leave.

Just then Sandi knocked on the door to announce that Tiffany's parents had come to pick her up. Opening that door was one of the hardest things she'd ever done. She'd made such a complete fool of herself that she didn't want to face her classmates. Furthermore, what would her parents say and how could she ever explain?

Instead of scolding her, Tiffany's father prayed with her and gave her a Bible verse: "For where you have envy and selfish ambition, there you find disorder and every evil practice" (James 3:16).

And that night Tiffany fell into the arms of Jesus, confessed her sin, took off her mask, and realized that only as Jesus lived His life in her could she be the person she was created to be—fulfilled, joyful, and "real."

But you don't have to learn this lesson the hard way, as Tiffany did. The formula for being your best is found in the Bible: "So then, just as you received Christ Jesus as Lord, continue to live in him, rooted and built up in him, strengthened in the faith as you were taught, and overflowing with thanksgiving. See to it that no one takes you captive through hollow and deceptive philosophy, which depends on human tradition and the basic principles of this world rather than on Christ. For in Christ all the fullness of the Deity lives in bodily form, and you have been given fullness in Christ" (Col. 2:6–10). All you have to do is believe God's Word and live by it. You don't have to repeat the humiliating experiment.

The Wrong Entry That Always Boggles Up the Program

Annette buried her head in her pillow and began to sob. Her father had been drinking again. For the hundredth time he had come home and screamed at her: "You're no good! You're a complete disappointment to me. You're a nervous wreck and your grades are terrible. You'll never amount to anything!" Horrible memories rushed into her mind: the times he had spanked her for no reason when she was a little girl, the Christmas they had eaten chicken noodle soup because he had drunk up all the money, and two months ago when Jeff had come to pick her up for a date and her father's obnoxious behavior had ruined the whole evening for her. Waves of self-pity engulfed her. Bitterness and anger welled up from deep inside. She felt as though her wounds were too deep to be healed, and it was all her father's fault. When she tried to pray, God seemed a million miles away.

Have you ever experienced a similar scene in your life? Is there someone you think you can't forgive? If you believe that lie, you'll be a prisoner for life. "Forgiveness is not a feeling; it is a rational decision, an act of the will. Our act of forgiving is compliance with God's command. God says that if we expect His forgiveness, we must be forgiving. If we choose not to forgive, we can expect to be tormented until we do."[1]

---

[1]Frank D. Hammond, *Overcoming Rejection* (Plainview, Tex.: The Children's Bread Ministry, 1987).

It's a spiritual principle that you'll never be free until you forgive. It's also true that on your own strength, you won't be able to muster up the ability to forgive. But when you say, "Lord, I forgive—my mother, my teacher, or Susie—by faith (no matter how I feel and in spite of my screaming emotions) and I believe that you'll change me," God works a miracle in you. Your willingness to let God work in you causes a miracle to occur. Power to forgive and to love your enemies is a true "class-*A* miracle," one you can experience today. And God's miracles are always a lot of fun.

The devil will constantly try to use unforgiveness to erode your true personality in Jesus. God's purpose for you is that the "Lord Jesus be glorified in you, and you in him" (2 Thess. 1:12). But in order for this to happen, you must forgive everyone—all the time, right away, no matter what. Unforgiveness is the wrong entry that always boggles up the program.

VISUALIZE UNFORGIVENESS

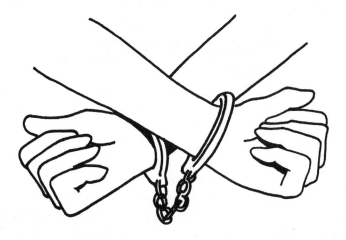

MEMORIZE

"Be kind and compassionate to one another, forgiving each other, just as in Christ God forgave you" (Eph. 4:32).

PERSONALIZE

I will be kind and tenderhearted to other people. I will forgive them even if they don't deserve it because that's the way Jesus has forgiven me.

PRAY THE VERSE, APPLYING IT TO YOUR LIFE

Dear God, I determine by faith to show extra kindness and compassion to _____ . Show me something special I can do for him/her. I will forgive _____ because I get the power from Jesus and I'll obey His command. Thank you, Lord, for forgiving me—even if I don't deserve it—and for giving me the power to forgive.

DECIDE TO FORGIVE

Prayerfully make a list of people you haven't fully forgiven. After each name write out Eph. 4:32, adding the words "and I will forgive (person's name)." Will to forgive, disregarding your emotions.

Misery Guarantee

Valerie was a straight *A* student. The counselor had just called her into his office to inform her that she and two other classmates had 98.5 averages. The results of the semester exams would decide who would be valedictorian of the senior class. To Valerie, this honor was very important. Both of her parents had graduated at the top of their classes, so there was the family tradition to uphold. She also thought that "valedictorian Val" had a nice ring to it.

Her big problem was fourth-year French. The new teacher who had replaced Mrs. Masterson was by far the hardest and the most unpopular teacher at Armstrong High. She constantly required that her students memorize and correctly spell incredibly long lists of vocabulary words. Valerie had trouble spelling all those words correctly and remembering where the accent marks went. She knew she could do well in her other subjects, but French really worried her. It just didn't seem fair. She was the only one of the three tied for top academic honors who had to suffer through French IV. If she'd only known what the new teacher was like, she would have chosen another course.

Suddenly an idea came to her. She was noted for her honesty and integrity, so no one would ever suspect *her* of copying. She could make a little crib sheet with the hardest words on it to double-check a word she was unsure of. It really wouldn't be cheating she reasoned, since she would study just as hard as if she didn't have the answers. Besides, it was the only way she could have an equal chance of competing with her rivals.

A verse she had learned in Sunday school came to her mind: "Be careful to do what is right in the eyes of everybody" (Rom. 12:17). But she brushed it aside with: "This is a special case, and I wouldn't even think of it if the teacher gave fair tests in the first place."

When the day of the test arrived, she placed a small kleenex pack on her desk as usual. Only the first kleenex contained her list of difficult words. During the exam, she peeked to check out the words she didn't remember, and no one seemed to notice. She breathed a sigh of relief as she handed in her test without getting caught.

But three days later, when the teacher congratulated her in front of the whole class for her perfect paper, she didn't feel very happy down inside. And she didn't even enjoy the day the office announced that she was class valedictorian. She politely accepted all the congratulations, but her heart wasn't in it. Somehow, she dreaded graduation night. Her dream of four years had suddenly lost its luster.

Are you a Valerie? Are you trying to live with unconfessed sin in your life? You'll never be at peace until you own up to it and make everything right. The psalmist David recounts his own experience:

> When I kept silent, my bones wasted away through my groaning all day long. For day and night your hand was heavy upon me; my strength was sapped as in the heat of summer. Then I acknowledged my sin to you and did not cover up my iniquity. I said, "I will confess my transgressions to the Lord"—and you forgave the guilt of my sin. (Ps. 32:3–5)

Your story will be no different. An unrepentant heart guarantees you misery. You'll be an unhappy, unproductive Christian until you come clear. No matter what the cost, you must confess every sin, doing everything in your power to make things right. After that, receive God's complete forgiveness and the wonderful joy of your salvation. Don't let unconfessed sin hide the true personality you have in Jesus Christ.

MEMORIZE

"He who conceals his sins does not prosper, but whoever confesses them and renounces them finds mercy" (Prov. 28:13).

VISUALIZE

PERSONALIZE

I, _____ (your name), can't cover up any sins and expect God to bless me, but if I own up to my sins and turn away from them, I'll find forgiveness and peace.

PRAY THE VERSE, APPLYING IT TO YOUR LIFE

Dear God, search my heart. If I've covered up a lie or the theft of something little or the fact that I started an untrue rumor, or ____, I determine to confess it—no matter what it costs. I will stop sinning and receive your mercy and forgiveness. I will remember that I can't enjoy prosperity if there is unconfessed sin in my life. (DON'T PRAY THIS UNLESS YOU MEAN IT.)

MEDITATE ON SCRIPTURE

Make a duplicate of this card and carry it around with you today. Use each chance you get to spiritually digest this verse and make it part of your life. Go to sleep repeating Prov. 28:13 in your mind.

Unmasking the "Nobody's-Going-to-Tell-Me-What-to-Do" Thief

Rocky's parents sat him down in the living room, and his father solemnly began, "Son, we want to have a talk with you."

Rocky felt his muscles stiffen and mentally prepared his defensive strategy. He was nearly eighteen years old, and he didn't appreciate anyone else trying to run his life.

"Rocky," his mother continued, "you're very gifted intellectually, and there's no excuse for bringing home any C's on your report card. Your senior grades are very important for getting into a good college. You're about to blow everything. And you show the same irresponsibility around the house. It's your job to take out the garbage. If I hadn't intervened last week, the health department would have. I don't have adequate vocabulary to describe the condition of your room. I never dreamed that any part of *my* house could be such a disgrace."

"Besides," his father went on, "you could show your parents a little respect. I suppose that 'please' and 'thank you' and 'I'd be glad to help' are too old-fashioned to show up in your vocabulary. The way you treat your little sister is actually cruel.

"I want to see some changes—and you're not going to see the car keys until they occur. When I was a boy, I walked or took the bus. You can do the same."

Rocky's face flushed as he snapped back, "After seven more months I'll move out forever and the house will become a paradise! It's time you realized that I'm grown up and you can't treat me like a little kid anymore!" With that he left the room and went to call Pete to pick him up.

Have you ever been a Rocky in a similar scenario. Do you hate having someone boss you around? If so, you need to listen to something God says in His Word: "But the wisdom that comes from heaven is first of all pure, then peace loving, considerate, submissive, full of mercy and good fruit; impartial and sincere" (James 3:17). Because true wisdom is submissive, there's no place in a Christian for the "nobody's-going-to-tell-me-what-to-do" attitude. In fact, the Bible is even more specific: "Whoever loves discipline loves knowledge, but he who hates correction is stupid" (Prov. 12:1). Heavy duty stuff!

The devil tempts all young people to mar the personality Jesus planned for them by an unteachable spirit. God didn't make us to be self-sufficient beings. He created us to depend, first of all on Him, and then on the body of Christ. One of the easiest ways to ruin your life is to refuse to take advice from your parents, teachers, pastors, and other Christians. The "nobody's-going-to-tell-me-what-to-do" strategy is one of the devil's most effective methods for robbing you of God's blessings and keeping you from seeing His fantastic design for your personality. Unmask the thief and don't let him take anything from you.

MEMORIZE

"Plans fail for lack of counsel, but with many advisers they succeed" (Prov. 15:22).

PERSONALIZE

God's Word says that my plans will fail if I refuse to take advice. But if I have a teachable spirit and try to learn from others, I'll succeed.

PRAY THE VERSE, APPLYING IT TO YOUR LIFE

God, please forgive me for a nobody's-going-to-tell-me-what-to-do attitude, especially in regard to _____ and _____. I ask you to show me the people I should seek advice from. Thank you for your promise of success if I surround myself with many advisers.

START A STRATEGY FOR SUCCESS

List the decisions you must make soon. Besides seeking counsel from your parents (whether or not they are Christians), ask God to show you wise and godly people from whom you should accept advice. Make appointments to talk with these people.

Dishonesty in the Limelight

Donna was secretary of the teen board at her church. Dave, the president, was an excellent leader, but tact wasn't one of his strong points. When he interrupted her idea with, "That's totally ridiculous. Only a dumb blond could think of such a thing," it was like a knife going through her. Later when he asked her if he had offended her, she told him that everything was okay. Although it really was a lie, she actually didn't know how to say, "Yes, your remark really did hurt me." And instead of going to God for comfort, she blamed herself for not being strong and victorious, a Christian who could ignore all feelings and march on ahead just as if nothing had happened.

But because she buried her feelings and her needs, months later when Dave was giving orders to everyone, she came out with a snippy "Heil Hitler!" Even though she had mentally accused Dave of being a dictator, the words surprised her as much as anyone else. And, of course, she felt terrible.

Has anything like that ever happened to you? Most of us suffer the consequences of a deep-down dishonesty in some area of life. And often that deception has been taught to us as a virtue!

You may have learned that it is noble never to admit weakness or dependence on others. But it's really covering up the truth. Lying to avoid hurting another person's feelings or to keep the peace is still breaking one of God's Ten Commandments, and you'll suffer for it. Giving manufactured excuses instead of a clear no may seem like the polite thing to do. But it's being untruthful. Saying, "No, nothing's bothering me," instead of "I really can't talk about it now," is just another lie.

There are other ways in which people refuse to face truth. Some people are so defensive they have an automatic reflex that blames the weather, the person in authority, the dog, the traffic, or the person nearest them when anything might be construed to be their fault. That constant falsification takes its toll on their personal lives and on their friendships. Others live a lie either by exaggerating to get attention or actually fabricating some stories to make themselves look good. And there are those who make a "I-am-the-greatest cassette," so they can lie without thinking twice. When God convicts us of sin, we often turn on an automatic denial system and lose out on the blessings of true confessions and forgiveness.

Jesus offers us freedom from our imagined need to hide the truth. But first we must realize that fear of rejection often springs the dishonesty trap. We are afraid that rejection will follow the revelation of weakness. Anxiety reasons, "Nobody will want to listen to me if I don't spice up my weekend a little bit." Insecurity screams, "You can't take the blame or stop bragging about yourself because you've got to prove yourself to be superior if you're to be respected."

Bring your need for acceptance to Jesus. Receive His love and His power. Your prayer should be something like this: "Dear Lord, I can go bowling with the rest and expose my lack of athletic ability instead of making up another excuse because you accept me just the way I am and I can accept myself." Or, "Lord, I don't have to give untrue compliments just so people will like me. I receive from you all the love I need." Or, "Dear God, I can say, 'I'm sorry; it's my fault,' instead of transferring the blame, because you love me even if I'm not perfect. Your love enables me to acknowledge my mistakes."

Ask God to put the spotlight on dishonesty in your life. Receive your acceptance from God instead of from a fantasy you've constructed. Don't let any dishonesty keep you from being the person God created you to be.

VISUALIZE DISHONESTY

MEMORIZE

"Rather, we have renounced secret and shameful ways; we do not use deception" (2 Cor. 4:2).

PERSONALIZE

If I feel compelled to keep something a secret, there's a big chance that it's wrong. I must open myself to God's conviction. (This does NOT mean that you're to publicly confess every sin. You only confess to God and to the person or people you've sinned against.) I must ask God to expose deception in my life.

PRAY THE VERSE, APPLYING IT TO YOUR LIFE

Dear God, spotlight secret and shameful thoughts and actions in my life. I will stop doing anything that I'd rather not have other people know about. Help me rid my life of dishonesty and deception.

CLEAN OUT THE CLOSET OF YOUR LIFE

Make a list of the bad things you've done that nobody knows about. If you haven't already done so, confess them to God and to any person you've wronged. Then burn the paper. Now make a list of thoughts and actions you think or do on the sly. Determine to stop thinking and doing these things.

God at the Controls

Stunned, Jim sat behind the steering wheel of his parked car. What Ginny was telling him between sobs was more than he could digest. "Jim, I really care about you," she was saying as she moved closer to her door; "but I just can't date a guy who constantly uses his temper tantrums to get his own way. Trying to talk things over with you is like carrying on a conversation with an active volcano. I never know when you're going to explode.

"Sometimes," she continued, "I'm thoroughly embarrassed by your public outbursts. Other times you take out all your frustrations on me—whether or not I'm part of the problem. I've tried to give you a fair chance, but I just can't take it anymore."

At that, Ginny, who was usually so sweet and supportive, slammed the car door and ran into the house. Jim was hurt and confused. How could Ginny really feel that way about him? He sincerely loved her and thought he had gone out of his way to show how much he cared. He knew he had a short fuse, just like everyone in his family. But he just couldn't understand why she became so upset by his anger.

Finally, Jim went to his youth pastor and received some godly advice. "Jim," his pastor counseled, "we're usually blind to our own worst faults—so blind that we don't consider them as sins even if the Bible says they are wrong. One of the fruits of the Spirit is self-control and it is listed in 2 Peter, chapter one, as a necessary foundation for love. When our emotions get out of control, we're not walking in the Spirit. But instead of getting caught up in personality differences and what kinds of emotional expressions are legitimate, let's get to the root of the problem.

"We get angry because we want to control people and situations. Instead of letting God handle things, we attempt to take charge ourselves. If Paul is late or Cherry forgets to return the borrowed book, anger signals that a repeat performance will not be tolerated. Although blowing up at a traffic jam will change nothing, it creates the illusion that we have some authority.

"If you refuse to accept people as they are—irresponsible, overly talkative, lazy, unthoughtful, or sloppy—and consistently show your irritations each time they violate one of *your* standards, people will feel inadequate and uncomfortable around you. If each mistake is greeted with angry scolding, people become afraid of you or they give up trying to please you.

"To be the person God created you to be, you have to stop impersonating God. 'Be still and know that I am God' (Ps. 46:10) can come to your rescue daily. It's true that other sins also have their roots in our refusing to entrust everything and everyone totally to God's care, but anger probably hurts other people the most.

"So when you miss the bus or drop the ketchup, just let God take over so you can relax and be the you God had in mind in His blueprints. If Judy doesn't keep your secret or Tim steals your assignment, don't let your anger mar the true personality God gave you. Put yourself under God's protection and ask Him to take charge. With God at the controls, your true personality can blossom without the blighting effects of anger, irritation, and temper tantrums."

YOUR LIFE CAN CHANGE

MEMORIZE

"Refrain from anger and turn from wrath; do not fret—it leads only to evil" (Ps. 37:8).

PERSONALIZE

I, _____ , will allow God to be at the controls of my life so I can give up anger, irritation, and worry. I know that these things will only cause me trouble.

PRAY THE VERSE, APPLYING IT TO YOUR LIFE

Dear God, I ask you to help me not to be angry about _____ and _____ . Help me not to worry about _____ . Help me to see that anger and worry only cause more problems.

ATTACK ANGER

Make a list of the things which most frequently make you angry. Then explain how deciding not to try to control the situation or the person could defuse that anger. Tell how letting God take care of everything could give you peace. Keep this list. When you actually face the problem situation without anger because you let God take charge, check it off and describe what happened.

Measuring Up

Tracy's alarm clock announced the beginning of a new day, but she wasn't at all thrilled by the prospect. In some ways she felt like a slave working for many masters: teachers, parents, bosses, and peers. She worked for hours each week to write a theme good enough to receive an *A* from Miss Johnson. Chemistry was worse. No matter what she did—and Tracy even stayed up all night to study for one test—she couldn't get above a *B*. And for Tracy that big *B* on her otherwise straight *A* report card said, "Tracy, you're not good enough." When Mr. Black gave his "students-aren't-as-good-as-they-used-to-be" speeches, Tracy wondered what made her inferior.

But it wasn't just another day of competition at school that she dreaded. The problem went deeper. For Tracy, being a member of the girls' volleyball team was anything but relaxing. She was determined to be the best. If she messed up on her serve or failed to return the ball, she considered it a major disaster. Precise and somewhat demanding, Tracy's father often corrected her. It was Tracy's goal to do everything right the first time so that her father would be pleased with her, but she seldom succeeded. Fast food order clerk at Burger King, she attempted to be accurate and efficient, but she was noticed by the manager only when she did something wrong. She tried desperately to wear the right clothes, to say the right things, and in every way possible to win the acceptance of her friends. Tracy's theology was that God expected her to do her best and that *A's* and first place and commendation from other people were proof that she had succeeded.

Then one Sunday morning as she was planning her week's schedule during the pastor's sermon, she allowed herself to be interrupted with these words: "Do you really know what God expects of you? Or have you been making up your own standards? Well, God tells us what He wants from us. Micah 6:8 reads: "And what does the Lord require of you? To act justly and to love mercy and to walk humbly with your God."

"Notice," the pastor continued, "that God says nothing about winning, about being the best, or about receiving high ratings from your supervisor. God asks you to 'act justly.' That means that you please God only—you work hard, you're fair, your motives are pure, and you don't permit some false earthly standards to be the measure of your value. You show compassion, you think about others and care about them so much that you keep the spotlight off yourself. And you 'walk humbly with your God.' You spend quality time with Jesus. Because you realize that He is all-powerful and all-knowing, you submit yourself totally to Him. Then you can stop striving and start living the Jesus life. This is the only way you can become the person God saved you to be."

That morning Tracy made a discovery. Jesus didn't expect her to get *A's* in chemistry. He didn't require that she never fail to meet her father's standards of preciseness. The Lord always noticed her good work. She responded by asking forgiveness for trying to set God's standards for Him and left her pressure cooker behind as she walked out into the sunshine of God's love. Tracy realized that she could stop trying so hard and relax in the presence of Jesus. Constantly receiving from Jesus, she could let her true personality reflect God's glory.

Maybe you, like Tracy, have been trying to measure up to the wrong standard. If so, determine right now that prayerful study of the Scriptures will free you to live by God's yardstick.

MEMORIZE

"Love the Lord your God with all your heart and with all your soul and with all your strength and with all your mind, and love your neighbor as yourself" (Luke 10:27).

VISUALIZE

PERSONALIZE

I will love God more than anyone else and more than anything else. I have made up my mind that He deserves the best I have. And I will love other people as much as I love myself. I will not replace His standards with my own.

PRAY THE VERSE, APPLYING IT TO YOUR LIFE

Dear God: I promise to love you more than _____ . Help me to concentrate all my efforts on showing you that I love you by obeying you. Give me your love for other people so I can love them as much as I love myself.

MEDITATE ON SCRIPTURE

Make a copy of this card to take along with you. Use every opportunity today to think about this verse and apply it to your life. Go to sleep meditating on this verse.

An Inferiority Complex With Two Heads

Holly sat down at the counter stool and watched her mom as she rolled out the crust for her famous homemade pizza. Then she began to pour out her heart. "Mom," she began, "I wish our church wasn't so small and that there was someone else to hang around with besides Laurel. She's always putting other people down in order to make herself look good. She's told me that I sing off key, that I have terrible study habits, that I'm a mama's baby, that I dress out of style, and that I don't witness as well as she does. Besides, she criticizes almost everyone we know—and it's usually followed by a comment assuring me that she is far superior to the poor soul she's accusing. I just can't stand to be around her."

"Holly," her mom began gently, "have you ever wondered *why* Laurel talks like that?"

"I suppose it's because she's proud and feels she's better than everyone else," Holly replied.

"I don't think you really know your friend," her mother counseled. "I see Laurel as a very insecure girl who tries to cover up her feelings of inferiority by bragging and putting others down. Don't take me wrong, but you're both a lot alike. It's just that you wear your inferiority complex on your sleeve. Timidity, caution, super-sensitivity, constant need for encouragement, and trying too hard to do *everything* right are the signals you send out.

You two are different sides of the same coin."

The devil constantly tries to make us insecure, to tell us we're not good enough, and to force us to try to defend ourselves and to prove our worth. He knows that a dose of inferiority has enough poison in it to make an otherwise healthy Christian personality a little sick. Swallowing great quantities of the "you-don't-measure-up-and-there-fore-you're-a-failure" virus can camouflage the fruits of the Holy Spirit so successfully that others hardly notice them.

The cure is believing what God says about you. You're His special design for His specific purpose. What the Lord said to Jeremiah, He's saying to you: "Before I formed you in the womb, I knew you: before you were born I set you apart" (Jer. 1:5). There's no limit to what the power of the Holy Spirit can do in you—if you only permit Him to be himself in you. He's constantly working to erase the scars and hurts that have messed you up. "He who began a good work in you will carry it on to completion until the day of Christ Jesus" (Phil. 1:6). And He'll love you and stick with you forever. "Never will I leave you, never will I forsake you" (Heb. 13:5) is His promise. Determining to believe God's truth every minute of every day is the antidote for Satan's poison. Don't let TV commercials, *Seventeen* magazine, or Billie Jane's comment convince you you're inferior and erode the personality you have in Jesus Christ.

VISUALIZE INFERIORITY

MEMORIZE

"Yet if you devote your heart to him . . . you will be secure, because there is hope" (Job 11:13,18).

PERSONALIZE

In spite of _____ , _____ , and _____ , I can give my whole heart to Jesus and find security because there is hope in Him.

PRAY THE VERSE, APPLYING IT TO YOUR LIFE

Dear God, I devote my heart to you, even _____ (something you often want to hang on to). I trust you to give me security because I'm putting my hope in you.

GETTING YOUR SECURITY FROM GOD

What do you need most—a good friend, an adult who will love you and give you Christian counsel, Christian fun? Ask God to fulfill this need and to supply it in *His way*.

WEEK 3
DAY 1

Self-Examination

1. Is there any way you've been compromising your testimony in order to impress the other kids? _no_ Confess it to God and determine to change.

2. There are some people I'll never be able to forgive.

    T (F)

3. I can WILL to forgive everyone and trust God to work a miracle in me so that forgiveness becomes real.

    (T) F

4. Which verse are you going to internalize to help you forgive?

    _____ a. Matt. 6:14–15.
    _✓_ b. Eph. 4:32.
    _____ c. Gal. 6:1.
    _✓_ d. Other _____ (specify).

    (Make a card with the verse on it and start memorizing it right now.)

5. He who hates correction is _stupid_ (Prov. 12:1).

6. What dishonesty have you discovered in your life?

    _____ a. Lying to make people feel better or to keep the peace.
    _____ b. Automatically blaming others for your mistakes.
    _✓_ c. Exaggerating to get attention.
    _✓_ d. Other (specify) _Lying to people (friends)_

44

7. What is always guaranteed to make you miserable?
    ____ a. Cloudy days.
    ____ b. Unfair tests.
    ____ c. Unconfessed sin.
    ____ d. Losing the game.

8. What thought can rescue me when I'm tempted to get angry at my teacher for giving a hard test or to blow up at my little sister for breaking my calculator?
    ____ a. Be still and know that I am God.
    ____ b. I must vent my emotions so I can feel better.
    ____ c. It's important to scold people so they remember not to do it again.
    ____ d. All of the above.

9. What is God's standard?
    ____ a. Play to win.
    ____ b. Act justly, love mercy, walk humbly with God.
    ____ c. Be the best in everything.
    ____ d. God helps those who help themselves.

10. What is the cure for insecurity? _Believing god. me._

PART 2

In Jesus I Am a Winner

In all these things we are more than conquerors through him who loved us.

Romans 8:37

WEEK 3
DAY 2

Mashing That Mincemeat Mentality

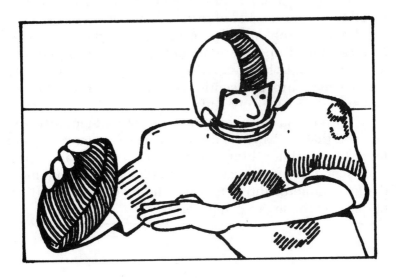

It was the football game of the season. The experts agreed that no other team in the conference was capable of defeating either of them. So, this was the game that would decide the city championship. Both teams looked forward to the game. And finally there they were, playing their hearts out.

At the beginning of the fourth quarter, a field goal tied the score. Excitement mounted. Late in that quarter, Eisenhower High made three first-downs in a row. When their quarterback threw a completed touchdown pass with only 51 seconds left in the game, Eisenhower fans went wild. As the clock ran out, pandemonium broke loose. There's nothing in the world quite like winning.

Somehow there are a lot of Christians who don't approach spiritual battles with similar gusto. A kind of "the-devil-will-make-mincemeat-out-of-me" mentality prevails. "If I can only make it through the day" and "I can't wait for the weekend" come from the lips of Christians as well as from the mouths of unbelievers. But it doesn't have to be that way. New Testament Christians who took God's Word seriously lived in another dimension.

In Rom. 8:37 we find these words: "No, in ALL these things we are more than conquerors through him who loved us." And the list of things that precedes this statement makes problems like boring classes, dateless weekends, a banged-up car and parents who don't understand look pretty pale by comparison. Included in his list are trouble, hardship, persecution, famine, nakedness, danger and sword! Heavy duty stuff!

It's time you dumped that mincemeat mentality and decided that God's Word is really true—for you. Say it out loud: "In all these things—a brother on drugs, an impossible schedule, an unreasonable math teacher—I am more than a conqueror through Jesus who loved me." Start experiencing the joy of being a winner.

Onward Christian Cream Puffs

What picture comes to your mind when you think of a winner?

Do you see a smiling track star brushing a wisp of unruly blond hair off his forehead as he repeats some humble-sounding words over the microphone, shakes the hand of the coach and receives his trophy? Or do you visualize hours of hard training, turning down pizza before the track meet, getting up at 5:00 A.M. to go on a long run before getting ready for school and staying on the team even when his girlfriend gave him an ultimatum—("It's either me or the track team!"). Do you imagine that Central High's football team just happened to go undefeated all season? Or do you look back to sweaty boys practicing day after day under the sweltering August sun, the pain of torn muscles, and the discipline of sticking by the training rules?

It might seem strange, but winning and suffering go together. The Apostle Paul knew that and he said, "I want to know Christ and the power of his resurrection and the fellowship of sharing in his sufferings" (Phil. 3:10).

Paul got that opportunity. He was willing to suffer in order to win and he had the attitude of a champion during his suffering.

He was one of God's winners. In Jesus, you too are a winner—a victorious Christian life is available to you, but that doesn't mean smooth sailing and trouble-free driving from here to eternity.

Let's look in on what happened to Paul. Beaten and put into prison unjustly, he acted every bit like a winner. Knowing that he served a God who never lost a tournament, he organized a midnight pep rally. He and Silas sang praises to the Lord, God sent an earthquake, and soon they were free. Paul was probably so happy that he didn't even notice his sore back.

This was not the only problem Paul ever faced. As a passenger on a ship during a terrible storm, he trusted God. One night God sent His angel to assure Paul that his life and the lives of those who traveled with him would be saved, even though the ship would be lost. Paul announced this to everyone and proceeded to take charge— certainly one of the few men in history to organize a successful shipwreck! Even in the suffering of being a prisoner, Paul was not a victim. He witnessed to all his guards, and ended his life on this note: "I have fought the good fight, I have finished the race, I have kept the faith" (2 Tim. 4:7).

Because you are in Jesus, you play on the winning team. The power of Jesus within you gives you the capacity to triumph in every situation. But you can just sit on the bench and watch other Christians suffer, fight and win. Or you can be a full participant. Winning and suffering go together, but the winning is wonderful.

Don't ever forget that it's "onward Christian soldiers," not "onward Christian cream puffs!"

MEMORIZE

"Let us fix our eyes on Jesus, the author and perfecter of our faith, who for the joy set before him endured the cross, scorning its shame, and sat down at the right hand of the throne of God" (Heb. 12:2).

VISUALIZE

PERSONALIZE

I will put my eyes on Jesus, the author and perfecter of my faith. I will remember the example of Jesus who, because of the joy set before Him, endured the cross and now is sitting at the right hand of the throne of God.

PRAY THE VERSE, APPLYING IT TO YOUR LIFE

Dear God, help me fix my eyes on Jesus, the author and perfecter of my faith, and not on _____ (current problem). Lord, help me remember how Jesus endured the cross because He saw His future glory at the right hand of the throne of God. Help me face _____ (current problem) with a winner's attitude and see your victory at the end.

MEDITATE ON SCRIPTURE

Duplicate this card and carry it around all day. Keep your mind on this verse and let it change you. Fall asleep with its words running through your head.

The Invisible Victory

Perhaps you're saying to yourself, "Hey, don't give me any of this theoretical stuff about being a winner. Right now I'm defeated and I know it. I don't get along with my parents. I'm afraid to witness for Jesus at school; my grades are bad. And I've even thought of going back to drugs."

Okay. But just remember one thing: If the devil can get your eyes on difficult circumstances rather than on Jesus, you will live in defeat even though the resources for victory are at your disposal.

You could afford to learn a lesson from a famous World War II hero, Brigadier General Antony McAuliffe. It was late 1944 and U.S. military leaders knew that Hitler's defeat was certain; it was only a matter of time. Hitler, however, wanted another victory and concocted a scheme so unlikely that, for a while, it worked. He chose several German soldiers who spoke good English and had them dress in American uniforms. Road signs were changed, and these Germans gave U.S. troops wrong directions. They walked straight into a trap. The surprise attack worked, and Hitler got his little victory, known in history as the Battle of the Bulge.

Although one American unit was entirely surrounded by German forces, its commander, Antony McAuliffe, knew the score. He recognized that the situation was only temporary and that U.S. troops not only had the capacity to rescue him but to win the war. In spite of the worst possible visible circumstances, his reply to the German demand to surrender was "Nuts!" His faith in an unseen reality made a successful rescue operation possible.

The devil will see to it that your life is full of "Battle-of-the-Bulge" situations. Maybe your mother wants a divorce, or your best friend really lets you down, or people in your church are fighting and creating a very tense atmosphere. God asks you not to waver, but to believe that He has the power to rescue you. In fact, in Ephesians, we are told three times to stand firm. It's kind of like God knows that this is not easy to remember when the situation looks hopeless. "Therefore put on the full armor of God, so that when the day of evil comes, you may be able to stand your ground, and after you have done everything, to stand. Stand firm then" (Eph. 6:13–14).

A winner from Jesus' team knows that he or she is victorious even if it looks as if all is lost. Because God acts in response to our faith, it is not a matter of living through the day but of expecting the victory even when nothing but defeat can be seen.

When General McAuliffe said "nuts" to the surrender demand, he won an invisible victory. Nothing in his circumstances had changed, but he had made the decision that would make help possible. By faith, win some invisible victories right now. Then let God bring them into reality.

MEMORIZE

"Do not be afraid. Stand firm and you will see the deliverance the Lord will bring you today. The Egyptians you see today you will never see again" (Ex. 14:13).

VISUALIZE

PERSONALIZE

I will not be afraid of _____ (worry you have). I will stand firm and will see the deliverance the Lord will bring me today. (Often today's deliverance is freeing you from the fear, which paves the way for a change in circumstances later.) My "Egyptians" _____ (current big problems I see today), I'll never see again.

PRAY THE VERSE, APPLYING IT TO YOUR LIFE

Dear God, thank you that I don't have to be afraid of _____ . Thank you that you can give me power to stand firm and that you can deliver me. Thank you, Lord, that I will never see these "Egyptians" ____ (problems ready to attack you) as an impossibility again. Thank you for my invisible victory over them, which will pave the way for your miracle.

WIN SOME INSIVIBLE VICTORIES

Make a list of areas where you are wavering (e.g., I've about given up on praying for my dad's salvation). With a red pen, write over each item on your list: "I will stand firm and see the deliverance the Lord will bring me today. The _____ (specify your 'Egyptians') I see today, I will never see again."

Follow the Leader

You've probably experienced the same thing yourself. Tanya heard a super sermon about trusting God in everyday circumstances and she decided to put it into practice. Naturally the nervous type, she had worried a lot about her solo in the Christmas concert. But now she decided to claim, "So do not fear, for I am with you" (Isa. 41:16), and to really believe God meant what He said. When the big night came, she chased the butterflies from her stomach by firmly standing on that verse. Instead of fear, she felt God's presence, and she sang with joy and confidence.

Elated by her victory, she forgot to prepare spiritually for her next performance. Fear again overcame her. Once on the platform, her knees began to shake. She even forgot the words of the second verse. Mortified, she took her seat and tears filled her eyes.

Tanya had failed to remember that only *IN JESUS* are we winners. In 2 Cor. 2:14 we find the secret: "But thanks be to God, who always leads us in triumphal procession in Christ and through us spreads everywhere the fragrance of the knowledge of him." Jesus *ALWAYS* leads us in a victory parade—it's just that so often we don't follow.

Obviously, you must keep your eyes on your leader, or you'll lose him. Your eyes have to be on Jesus, not on your fear of failure or what other people think. Unless you are constantly meditating on God's Word and praying, your mind will wander in many directions. Whenever you face a challenge, prepare for it spiritually.

If someone is dating the boy or girl you like, take a good dose of Gal. 5:19–20: "Now the works of the flesh are plain: immorality, impurity, lasciviousness, idolatry, sorcery, enmity, strife, *JEALOUSY*, anger, selfishness, dissensions, party spirit, envy, drunkenness, carousing, orgies, and the like." If your mom is having a frustrating year and taking it all out on you, Ps. 27:10 can be your fortress: "Though my father and mother forsake me, the Lord will receive me." Keep on believing that God will provide for you what your mother is unable to give. Jesus makes His new creatures out of victory material, but you must cooperate with Him, or your potential won't be realized.

Then, too, following another person requires willingness to do things his way. The Lord's definition of victory might be different from yours. We'd like to push away every problem with one sweep, but God reminds us, "Better a patient man than a warrior, a man who controls his temper than one who takes a city" (Prov. 16:32). *YOU* can walk in victory through what may seem like total disaster.

"Follow the leader" is a game designed for kids—after all, if you're older, you want to call your own shots. However, refusing to do things Jesus' way will spell spiritual defeat for you. God always leads us in triumphal procession in Christ, but we must follow the leader.

MEMORIZE

"But thanks be to God! He gives us the victory through our Lord Jesus Christ" (1 Cor. 15:57).

VISUALIZE

PERSONALIZE

I give thanks to God. He gives victory through Jesus Christ, who is Lord.

PRAY THE VERSE, APPLYING IT TO YOUR LIFE

Dear God, I want to thank you for everything. Thank you, Lord, that you give me victory in _____ (current problem) through Jesus my Lord.

WRITE A THANK-YOU LETTER TO GOD

List every difficulty you face in this manner: Thank you, God, for the victory over fear of taking tests. Thank you, God, for the victory in learning to love my little sister.

Winning Is a Choice

How can you lose when you have an invincible weapon? Well, it's possible.

Watchman Nee tells how the Chinese fought against Japanese tanks in World War II. How can infantry men with rifles stand against modern tanks? Well, they figured out an effective strategy. In the closed turret of the tank, nothing could harm the Japanese driver. However, if he could be enticed to stick his head out, he could be shot just like anyone else. Chinese soldiers would hide in areas surrounding the tanks and fire single shots, first from one direction and then from another. Inevitably, the tank driver's curiosity would get the better of him. Sticking his head out to see where the shots were coming from, he added himself to the casualty list.

Did you know that God gave you a tank to fight against the rifles of the devil and his demons? The Bible tells us that in Jesus we are invincible. "You, dear children, are from God and have overcome them, because the one who is in you is greater than the one who is in the world" (1 John 4:4). You have the "more-than-conqueror" power of the Holy Spirit within you.

However, the devil has a number of ways of keeping you from depending on that dynamite power of God's Spirit within you. He tries to keep you ignorant about the full potential of that power within you. Don't fall for it. Do a Bible study on the Holy Spirit and let each verse speak to you. Remember that His power isn't just for other people. It's for you.

Satan will try to make you forget about the power available to you. During emergency and pressure situations, it's easy to simply react according to established patterns rather than to rely on the wisdom and the power of the Holy Spirit. Then the devil uses curiosity—getting you to stick your head out from under the protection God provided for those who obey Him. Don't ever read a dirty book, experiment with drugs, or go to a wild party just to find out what it's like. There are a lot of things you can afford to live without.

Another of Satan's tricks is to use exhaustion and frustration to weaken you to the point that you're willing to act impetuously instead of waiting for God's way and relying on His power. Ground yourself in God's Word so you don't fall for any of this nonsense.

God gave Jeremiah a promise that you must put in your arsenal: "Today I have made you a fortified city, an iron pillar and a bronze wall to stand against the whole land— against the kings of Judah, its officials, its priests, and the people of the land. They will fight against you but they will not overcome you, for I am with you and will rescue you" (Jer. 1:18–19). As long as Jeremiah trusted God and spoke His words to the people, he fit that description. When he forgot about the power within, he turned into a pessimist and a crybaby. How could Jeremiah bravely stand up in front of the priest, who had ordered him beaten and placed in stocks, to fearlessly proclaim God's truth—then a few minutes later cry out, "Cursed be the day I was born"? One minute Jeremiah was receiving all his power from the Holy Spirit, which made him every inch a winner. The next he became a practicing atheist, acting as if God were powerless.

We all see ourselves in Jeremiah. Each minute you make the decision: Will you stay safe inside the turret relying on God's power? Will you choose to be a winner? Or do you elect to go out on your own into loser's territory?

Winning is a choice.

VISUALIZE WRONG CHOICES

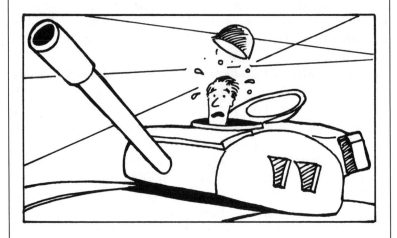

MEMORIZE

"You, dear children, are from God and have overcome them, because the one who is in you is greater than the one who is in the world" (1 John 4:4).

PERSONALIZE

I, _____ , am from God and have overcome the influences of Satan, because greater is the Holy Spirit in me than the power of the devil in the world.

PRAY THE VERSE, APPLYING IT TO YOUR LIFE

Dear God, thank you that I am from you and I have overcome the forces of evil like _____ (present situation). Thank you that your power in me is greater than any power that the devil has.

MAKE YOUR DREAM A REALITY

Write a description of the new you spending a victorious day at school letting the Jesus in you handle things, like the unfair assignment, the dirty jokes at the lunch table, and boring lectures. Then let Jesus make your dream come true.

I Shall Overcome—I Have Jesus' Power

The scene is familiar—the annual marathon race in Boston or Doomsburg or Pine City. Television cameras are in place and announcers are giving bio-data on famous runners who have come to participate. Someone will have to be first, but most people have only one goal: to cross the finish line. Everyone knows there'll be a lot of dropouts. Never having trained for it in the first place, some will receive frantic signals from their bodies that they had better quit. But a whole group of winners will cross the finish line with the satisfaction of having accomplished their objective.

The Apostle Paul reminds us: "Do you not know that in a race all the runners run, but only one gets the prize? Run in such a way as to get the prize" (1 Cor. 9:24). A winner needs to have his goal firmly in mind. Do you? Do you aim not only to get to heaven yourself but to take a whole bunch of other people with you? Are you willing to train, to sacrifice, to suffer, and to take sufficient time to study the Bible and to listen to instructions from the Holy Spirit so that your purpose can be realized? Do you want to win the prize Paul was talking about?

A winner must be an overcomer, because he or she won't be able to reach the goal without surmounting a lot of obstacles. First you'll encounter the test of priorities. You can get so easily sidetracked—having just the right clothes, skiing, or surfing, or bowling, or just working too many hours can take all your time and energy. Ask God what He wants to do with each day.

After you let God decide what things are important for you to do, the devil will design a new set of problems—your peers may tease you and reject you, your family may think you're some kind of a religious fanatic, or circumstances may appear most unfavorable.

But you can't afford to be Larry Loser who tries to be a Secret Service Christian so nobody at school will find out. You can't just drop your standards whenever it's convenient and open your Bible only during emergencies. The stakes are too high. You have only one life. You must decide to let Jesus make you a winner.

The book of Revelation sums it up best. After a beautiful description of heaven, these verses follow: "He who overcomes will inherit all this, and I will be his God and he will be my son. But the cowardly, the unbelieving, the vile, the murderers, the sexually immoral, those who practice magic arts, the idolaters, and all liars—their place will be in the fiery lake of burning sulfur. This is the second death" (Rev. 21:7–8). Being an overcomer is not an optional extra. It's an absolute necessity.

MEMORIZE

"Be faithful, even to the point of death, and I will give you the crown of life . . . He who overcomes will not be hurt at all by the second death" (Rev. 2:10–11).

VISUALIZE

PERSONALIZE

I want to be faithful to Jesus always—even to the point of death so Jesus can give me the crown of life. I want to be an overcomer so I won't be hurt at all by the second death. Heaven is my goal.

PRAY THE VERSE, APPLYING IT TO YOUR LIFE

Dear God, I receive your power to be faithful, even to the point of death. I'm looking forward to the crown of life. I receive your power to become an overcomer so I won't go to hell.

ELIMINATE LOSER'S LUGGAGE

Read Rev. 21:8 again. Are there some things you must permit Jesus to eradicate from your life? You can't be victorious unless you first identify the areas that you must let Jesus, the Overcomer, totally transform.

The Faith Connection

Reading through the Bible, you meet a lot of winners—members of the faith hall of fame. There's Moses at the Red Sea, Gideon and his 300, David facing Goliath, Daniel in the lions' den, Paul and Silas in prison, and Stephen being stoned. God displays His power and the Red Sea opens; confusion in the enemy camp enables Gideon and his men to win without fighting; Goliath is vanquished; Daniel is unhurt; an earthquake opens prison doors; and Stephen goes off to heaven, his face shining like an angel's.

Faith is the common ingredient found in all these victories. You need some of that overcoming faith in your own life.

Take that upcoming job interview, for instance. The disastrous memory of the last one fresh in your mind, you're dreading the appointment. You can't forget that sleepless night in which you rehearsed what you were going to say over and over again. Because of your nervousness, the words just wouldn't come out right. The interviewer finally interrupted: "I think you'd be happier in a job where you didn't have to constantly meet the public." And that was that.

This is the kind of situation that gives you the perfect opportunity to get to know the God of Moses, Gideon, David, Daniel, and Paul. Moses could have surrendered to Pharaoh's army; Gideon could have run away; David could have let someone else volunteer to fight the giant; Daniel could have prayed in secret; and Paul could have groaned and complained all night. These men weren't different from you and me—we're all made out of the same stuff. God hasn't changed either. He's just the same today as He always was. The secret is finding the faith connection and plugging in.

You can take the advice of the Apostle Paul: "Forgetting what is behind and straining toward what is ahead, I press on toward the goal" (Phil. 3:13–14). You can line yourself up with Heb. 11:6: "And without faith it is impossible to please God, because anyone who comes to him must believe that he exists *and that he rewards those who earnestly seek him.*" Do you really believe that God gives victories to those who want Him worse than anything else? Are you sure that God takes charge of the situations we truly turn over to Him? If God rewards those who diligently look for Him, your job interview will turn out differently if you take the time and effort to find the faith connection.

Because all of us must break through layers of habit, hypocrisy and ignorance, we must let God be the judge of our diligence in seeking Him. It's too easy for us to be like the first-grader who thinks that making two *W's* on his paper is his supreme penmanship effort, and if that isn't good enough, he'll just give up. Or we copy the Little Leaguer who cries because the long foul ball he hit doesn't count. We moan, "I really prayed about it, and everything went wrong."

The Bible says God *rewards* those who *earnestly* seek Him. You must believe that. In fact, you can't be a winner if you don't take that verse literally. God does give special prizes to those who search for Him with all their hearts. Acting on that promise is the key to the faith connection.

DOES THIS LOOK FAMILIAR?

MEMORIZE

"For everyone born of God has overcome the world. This is the victory that has overcome the world, even our faith" (1 John 5:4).

PERSONALIZE

I, _____ , am born of God and I can overcome the world. The victory that overcomes the world is my faith in Jesus.

PRAY THE VERSE, APPLYING IT TO YOUR LIFE

Dear God, thank you that because I am born of you, I can overcome _____ (problems facing you). My faith that you exist and that you reward those who earnestly seek you is the victory that overcomes the world.

MEDITATE ON SCRIPTURE

Meditate on this verse throughout the day. Go to sleep thinking about this verse.

Spark Plugs for Christians

Clark was totally discouraged. On Saturday night his youth leader had given him a pile of fliers for the city-wide rally. Enthusiastic about reaching the city for Christ, he, along with the others, volunteered to pass them out at school.

Yet the minute he had entered South High on Monday morning, he felt a strange fear well up within him. Timidly, he approached his friend John: "I know you may not be interested, but I'd like to give you an invitation to the rally next Saturday night."

Immediately John became defensive, "Leave me alone. I just can't believe that a straight *A* student like you could fall for such religious nonsense." Gulping, Clark managed a nervous, "You know—different strokes for different folks."

This encounter took the wind out of Clark's sails. The other fliers remained hidden inside his geometry book.

In contrast, Joe came home from school nearly walking on water. He had attended the same meeting Clark had, and also volunteered to pass out fliers. Entering the side door and heading toward his locker, he realized that the devil was trying to make him afraid. However, he remembered to apply God's truth to the situation. He quoted a Bible verse he had learned: "I have given you authority to trample on snakes and scorpions and to overcome all the power of the enemy" (Luke 10:19). When he started reasoning—"I have authority over the sneaky, snakey devil and his power, so I don't have to be afraid"—the fear left him.

"Barry," he said to a friend, "do you want to go to a rally Saturday night?"

"No," his friend shot back. "That's the *last* place on earth I'd spend a Saturday night. What do you think you are—a salesman for sinless Saturdays? Man, I'm out for a good time."

Joe still remembered he had authority and replied, "You're free to live your own life, but eternity is a terribly long time and you'd better get prepared for it."

The next two people Joe talked to were genuinely interested. Then along came Rusty, the captain of the football team—by far the most popular guy in school. Joe became tense and thought, *But I can't talk to him.* He missed his opportunity.

Realizing what had happened, he asked God to forgive him and rejected the condemnation the devil tried to put on him. He still had authority over Satan. He got a chance to witness to Blair at lunch, and by the end of the day had given out twenty-five fliers.

Joe had learned something very important. *Truth is power.* He had based his day on the truth found in God's Word, not on circumstances, as Clark had. He let the Holy Spirit apply God's Word to his life.

What would you think of a halfback who grounded the ball the minute it looked as if someone might tackle him? How would you view the fireman who, when he saw how big the blaze was, turned and left for home? The truth is, getting tackled doesn't kill a guy who's in good condition, and a fireman with proper training and equipment *can* put out a very big fire. Believing the right thing makes such a difference.

Truth is the spark plug you need to ignite the power of the Holy Spirit in you so you can live victoriously. The devil may say, "You've failed—you can't really witness to anybody anyway." But God's truth is: "Though a righteous man falls seven times, he rises again" (Prov. 24:16). Satan may whisper, "No one in your school even cares to hear about God." But truth answers, "Let us not become weary in doing good, for at the proper time we will reap a harvest if we do not give up" (Gal. 6:9).

So open your Bible. Truth is power, and you could use a few spark plugs.

VISUALIZE TRUTH AS POWERFUL

MEMORIZE

"Do not be overcome by evil, but overcome evil with good" (Rom. 12:21).

PERSONALIZE

I will not let the bad things get the best of me. By obeying God and receiving His power, I will overcome evil with good.

PRAY THE VERSE, APPLYING IT TO YOUR LIFE

Dear God, help me not to be blown away by all the evil around me and especially by _____ (evil close to you that bothers you). Show me what good things I can think about and do to conquer this evil and its effect on me.

START YOUR "OVERCOME EVIL WITH GOOD" CAMPAIGN TODAY

Ask God to give you His ideas for specific situations, then write them down; for example, My mom has been grouchy all week. It would be a good time to buy her flowers. I'm getting a *D* in algebra this quarter, but I'm going to go in after school for extra help until I understand all the work I missed.

Self-Examination

1. In what areas do you suffer from that "the-devil-is-going-to-make-mincemeat-out-of-me" mentality?____
   battles

2. Which verses are you going to internalize and use?
   ____ a. Rom. 8:37.
   ____ b. Josh. 1:9.
   ____ c. Prov. 28:1.
   ____ d. other (specify) _____.
      (Write this verse on a card and start memorizing it right now.)

3. Winning and suffering go together.   T̸ F

4. How do you win invisible victories?_____
   believe in God.

5. What do I have to remember if I'm to be a winner?
   all my power comes from Jesus.

6. Winners never mess things up.   T F̸

7. Winners fail sometimes, but know how to stand on God's truth and come back in victory.   T̸ F

8. ____*Truth*_____ is power.

9. Which of these things have been temptations to you this week?
   ____ a. Trying to be something I'm not;
   ____ b. Unwillingness to forgive;

70

_____ c. Reticence to own up to sin;

_____ d. Inability to take correction;

_____ e. Dishonesty in words or actions;

_____ f. Anger;

_____ g. Striving to prove my worth;

__✓__ h. Putting others down to make myself look good.

Did you remember that none of these things belong to the true personality Jesus gave you? Did you repent if you fell into one of those traps?

10. How can you beat an inferiority complex?_____

_____

1.–2. Personal. **3.** T. **4.** You take a stand in faith, believing God's Word although you SEE no change, thus making it possible for God to rescue you. **5.** All my power comes from Jesus, so I must constantly depend on Him and follow Him closely. **6.** F. **7.** T. **8.** Truth, the truth from God's Word. **9.** Personal. **10.** Determining to believe God's truth every moment of every day.

PART 3

In Jesus I Am Strong

Be strong in the Lord.

Ephesians 6:10

Tin Soldier Drops Out

"See you at Bible study tonight," greeted Sarah as she passed Dan in the hall.

"No you won't," Dan grunted. "I'm never coming back."

Sarah was so shocked that she forgot to stop at her locker to pick up her English theme. She didn't even hear the teacher's lecture on lower grades for late compositions. She was thinking about Dan. What had happened?

Dan had been a Christian for only six months, but he had witnessed to all his friends, had memorized more verses than anyone else and was considered the strongest Christian in school. There was no sign of weakness in him. How could Dan just give up?

What everybody didn't know was that Dan's father was an alcoholic, that his parents were getting a divorce, and that he had always covered up his insecurities by doing well in school, being a leader and excelling in sports. When he became a Christian, he decided to be the best. He had impressed everyone but he hadn't admitted his own deep needs. Hurting so much inside that he was sure his weaknesses would show, Dan just couldn't take off his mask. By quitting, he was still calling the shots—still in control. No one would ever know what the real Dan Anderson was like.

Dan didn't realize that the Christian army isn't made up of tin soldiers who never get hurt or have problems. It's composed of flesh-and-blood people who are strong *in the Lord* because they put on the full armor of God. A tin soldier needs no armor.

When David went to meet Goliath, he didn't try to hide his frailty and inexperience behind Saul's armor. David's weakness was exposed for all to see. Because of this, it was apparent to everyone that his strength came from God. If David had tried the I'm-hot-stuff-watch-instant-hero-in-action-God-is-for-losers routine, Goliath would have had another head for his trophy case. Instead, David just expected God to pour power into weakness—and He did. Because David had spent his spare time meditating on Scripture rather than playing "Frogger," he knew how to receive his strength from God.

Don't hide your weaknesses. Don't try to be a tin soldier. If you could be strong by yourself, the Bible wouldn't command, "Be strong in the Lord" (Eph. 6:10). If you had no weak spots, you'd need no armor. Use your weaknesses as an opportunity to receive extra strength from God instead of becoming a tin soldier drop out.

Just Admit You're a Minus Looking for a Plus

Daisy stared into the darkness. The digital dial on her snooze alarm blinked 1:20, but sleep was the furthest thing from her mind. She had expected a double-dose blessing from attending two Christian meetings in one day, but instead she had become thoroughly confused.

Daisy and four other girls had walked over to Colleen's apartment for Bible study on Friday after school as usual. Supportive and always kind, Colleen talked to them about being open about their problems, sharing their weaknesses and remembering that God is love. "We're all weak," Colleen had said, "but God loves us anyway, and He understands."

At 7:00 o'clock, Daisy and her friends went to hear a special speaker at Hope's church. The sermon was on enduring hardship and being a strong Christian. "Don't come up with any excuses. Don't say you're weak. The battle's too tough for sissies. You've got to be strong," thundered the man in the pulpit.

Hours later when everyone in her house was asleep, Daisy was still trying to sort things out. She reasoned, "If I don't admit my weaknesses, I'm a liar. But if I'm weak, I'm failing because I'm not a strong soldier."

Have you ever faced Daisy's dilemma? The Apostle Paul gives us the answer. "Therefore I will boast all the more gladly about my weaknesses, so that Christ's power may rest on me" (2 Cor. 12:9). Paul didn't just admit his weaknesses, he bragged about them. But he didn't make the mistake of misinterpreting them.

If certain people had written the Bible, they would have put, "Therefore I will boast all the more gladly about my weaknesses, so that others won't expect much of me because I'm a rather hopeless case. I really can't do much for God's kingdom." On the other hand, others would have written, "I put up a good front and never take off my 'I've-got-my-act-together' Christian mask, so that Christ's power may rest on me." But God wants neither weaklings who refuse His strength nor self-sufficient people who try to spread a little of God's power on top of human ability. It's kind of like the positive force of God's strength attracts our negatively charged weaknesses and the fusion of the two produces the same kind of stability and potential power that's found in the atom. If we try to neutralize the negatives of our insufficiency or ignore the positive of God's strength, the potential power of combining the two won't ever materialize.

Don't choose to be a self-propelled engine when you could become an atomic power plant. Just admit that you're a minus looking for a plus. Your weakness plus God's strength is dynamite!

MEMORIZE

"My grace is sufficient for you, for my power is made perfect in weakness. Therefore I will boast all the more gladly about my weaknesses, so that the power of Christ may rest on me" (2 Cor. 12:9).

VISUALIZE

PERSONALIZE

God's ability to give me all I need is good enough for me. Because God's power shows up best in my weaknesses, I won't try to hide them. I'll freely admit weaknesses, so like a magnet they can attract the power of Jesus.

PRAY THE VERSE, APPLYING IT TO YOUR LIFE

Thank you, God, that your grace is enough for me. I ask you that your power be shown in _____ (area of weakness). I won't hide _____ (another weakness) but will expect your power to rest on me.

MEDITATE ON SCRIPTURE

Take a card like this with you today. Find opportunities to hide this verse in your heart. Repeat its words as you fall asleep tonight.

No More Weak Ends!

It was still dark when Jody woke up. The clock on her dresser told her that it was 4:45 A.M., but she was too excited to sleep longer. This was her big day. The manager of Christian Recordings Incorporated had heard her solo and had invited her to come for an audition. Her appointment was for 9:00 A.M. Her father had promised to give her a ride since the recording studio was located in another part of the city.

They started out in plenty of time. However, after about forty minutes, they were driving along railroad tracks in the poorest section of the city. Jody's father had always boasted, "I know Chicago like the back of my hand." He didn't own a city map, and refused to ask anyone for directions. Jody's heart sank. She knew what her father was like when he didn't know where he was going. When they finally arrived at the studio an hour late, her father mumbled something about an accident on the freeway—failing to mention that it had nothing to do with their being late. Visibly shaken, Jody asked God for grace to forgive her father and for enough composure to sing her best.

It's pretty easy to see that Jody's father's refusal to admit a weakness and ask for help was costly. But it's a lot harder for each of us to see that there are areas in which we act just as he did. Underneath an unwillingness to admit weakness is fear. Sometimes we're afraid we'll fall apart if we admit to ourselves how weak we really feel. Other times we try to keep up appearances so no one will discover our inadequacies. And we cover it all up by pushiness, defensiveness, bragging and tearing others down to make ourselves look good.

And yet the cure is just as simple as asking for directions. If you really believe in an all-powerful God who can fill each weakness with His power, you just admit your inadequacies and *receive* His strength. The Bible commands us to "look to the Lord and his strength; seek his face always" (Ps. 105:4). We must continually confess our weaknesses and receive His strength.

This is only possible when we rest in Jesus and have so much faith in Him that we're afraid of nothing—even our weaknesses. The beginning isn't as important as the end. If you start out pretending you're strong, your weaknesses will soon show up. Admitting you need all the help God can give and receiving it by faith will eliminate the weak end.

MEMORIZE

"But we have this treasure in jars of clay to show that this all surpassing power is from God and not from us" (2 Cor. 4:7).

VISUALIZE

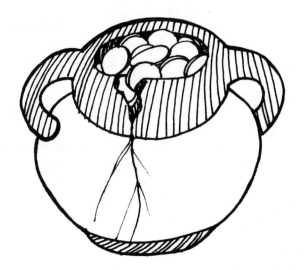

PERSONALIZE

I have the treasure of Jesus in me—a human full of weaknesses and defects—so that everyone will give God the credit instead of thinking I'm so great.

PRAY THE VERSE, APPLYING IT TO YOUR LIFE

Dear God, forgive me for sometimes trying to put on the pretense of being a golden vase instead of a jar of clay. Show me more and more how your wonderful power can show up in _____ (weakness that you have).

**LET YOUR WEAKNESSES BE PICTURE FRAMES
THAT DISPLAY THE STRENGTH OF JESUS**

Make a list of your deficiencies. After each item, write out 2 Cor. 4:7.

Are You a Crybaby Christian?

Dora loved Jesus with all her heart. She was very faithful in church, obedient to her parents, kind to others and diligent in school. But Dora had one very big problem that revealed itself by the constant use of two words in her conversation: "I can't."

Dora thought of herself as weak and inadequate. Whenever she was asked to do something, she'd reply, "I can't do it very well, but I'll try." She assumed that others were more capable than she, and always remained in the background. If she received a compliment, she'd reply, "It wasn't very good, but it was the best I could do."

As you can see, Dora had no problem admitting her weaknesses. It's just that she had no faith to expect God's power to more than make up for her deficiencies. She operated with an "expect-nothing-and-you'll-get-it-every-time" mentality. She didn't really believe that God was her strength, and maybe never even noticed that the Apostle Paul said, "When I am weak, then I am strong" (2 Cor. 12:10).

Have you swallowed any crybaby Christian myths? Have you played the "world-is-getting-so-wicked-that-all-Christians-can-do-is-hibernate-until-heaven" tune on your violin? Did you give up on winning your school for Jesus because the first ten people you talked to weren't interested? Have you decided that you can't learn good study habits, or stop overeating, or give up smoking pot? Are you in a prison of fear or self-consciousness or depression that is so confining you feel you can't escape?

If you are, you're the perfect place for the next miracle to happen! James tells us to count it all joy when we face trials, because they test our faith and teach us patience. Paul said he delighted in weaknesses, because in Christ he could get all the strength he needed. Gideon had a full-blown inferiority complex, but he was a scaredy-cat who opened his heart to receive God's strength. He and his three hundred men defeated a huge army without firing a gun, shooting an arrow, or even touching an enemy soldier.

It's about time you stopped being a crybaby Christian and really started asking God for strength in every area of weakness. "I can do everything through him who gives me strength" (Phil. 4:13). This is more than a memory verse that nearly everyone can quote: its truth is meant to touch you so deeply that crybaby changes to canbaby.

THE "I CAN'T DO IT" MENTALITY

MEMORIZE

"Have I not commanded you? Be strong and courageous. Do not be terrified; do not be discouraged, for the Lord your God will be with you wherever you go" (Josh. 1:9).

PERSONALIZE

I'd better listen to this command of God. He asks *me* to be strong and courageous, therefore I can trust Him to give me what it takes to conquer fear and discouragement. I will never forget that Jesus is with me no matter what.

PRAY THE VERSE, APPLYING IT TO YOUR LIFE

Dear God, with your help I will be strong and courageous. Thank you that I don't have to be scared of _____ because you're always there. Thank you that I don't have to be discouraged because you'll handle the problem of _____ for me.

CAPITALIZE ON A COMMAND

Write a paragraph on Josh. 1:9, answering these two questions: (1) Why can God command me, "Do not be terrified; do not be discouraged"? (2) How can I obey the command not to be terrified or discouraged?

The Rescue of Jack-in-a-box

As Jack sat down at his desk, he felt the weight of the world on his shoulders. Reviewing his schedule in his mind, he realized that he didn't even have time to sleep. He hadn't had his personal devotions in weeks.

Every day after school there was basketball practice. He went to Bible studies on Monday and Wednesday nights. There was a basketball game every Friday. Saturday he worked all day, and as Youth League president, he not only attended but planned the Saturday night meetings. He had to squeeze school assignments—and he was taking accelerated classes—into the spaces. It was already 10:00 P.M. and he was just starting his homework, which included a two-page English composition, the questions at the end of the chemistry chapter and preparing for a test in American History.

Worn out and discouraged, Jack put his head down on his desk and began to pray. Straight-A student, basketball star, spiritual giant on the outside, Jack was really weak and close to falling apart on the inside.

Have you ever felt like Jack? There are two things Jack needs to know—and they might come in handy for you as well.

First of all, the Bible says, "In repentance and rest is your salvation, in quietness and trust is your strength" (Isa. 30:15). If there is no time in your life for rest and quietness, you'll never be strong. Strength comes from the Lord, and if you're never still before Him, you'll never hear His voice. Part of the repentance (turning around and going in another direction) involved in receiving strength is in letting God revise your schedule. He will eliminate the things that keep you from spending time with Him. Rest also rebuilds us physically. I heard a very respected pastor say this: "You can be too physically tired to walk in the Spirit. When you lose all enthusiasm for your work and find yourself crabby and critical of others, the most spiritual thing you can do is get some extra sleep."

Don't ever forget: "In quietness and trust is your strength."

Secondly, you must learn that there are times when *God* calls you to do things that require supernatural strength. If you're obeying Him totally, you can cash in on the abundant supply of spiritual adrenalin available to God's servants. It's a promise: "He gives power to the faint, and to him who has no might he increases strength" (Isa. 40:29).

The Bible assures us that "they who wait for the Lord shall renew their strength." In Hebrew the prime root word for "wait" is "bind together." In order to revive your energy, you must take the time to bind yourself to Jesus. So many forces try to tear you away—excessive busyness, laziness, following *your* dreams instead of God's instructions, and marching in step with the world instead of listening to the heavenly cadence.

Sitting at his desk that night, Jack called out to God with a heart willing to obey. God showed him what to do: It was the *car* his grandmother had given him that required him to work Saturdays; if he sold it and used the money to pay for gas, he was free to borrow his mother's car. Having all day Saturday to catch up on sleep and homework would make his life manageable again. He also determined to get up earlier and spend time with God so he could take advantage of the extra strength that God gives to those who attach themselves to Him.

Jack-in-a-box was rescued by Jesus. Will you permit Him to deliver you?

READY TO BE RESCUED?

MEMORIZE

"But they who wait for the Lord shall renew their strength, they shall mount up with wings as eagles, they shall run and not be weary, they shall walk and not faint" (Isa. 40:31, RSV).

PERSONALIZE

If I get in step with Jesus, I'll get energy from a new source. Like an eagle I'll rise above my problems. I'll be able to depend on God's power to keep up the pace God has set for me without suffering exhaustion or burn out.

PRAY THE VERSE, APPLYING IT TO YOUR LIFE

Dear God, revise my schedule and renew my mind so I'm exactly on *your* wavelength. Lord, I open myself to receive your strength to soar above _____ (problem) and to keep on _____ (difficult thing you know God wants you to finish).

STOP RUNNING AHEAD AND WAIT FOR JESUS

Spend time with Jesus, receiving His opinion before making that date for Saturday night. Bind yourself to Jesus and receive His list of priorities for the day. Wait for instructions from Jesus before you spend your paycheck.

Walking on Water and Witnessing to "Barbie Doll"

Renee was just average—not outstanding in academics, sports, or music. She had a group of friends who sometimes referred to themselves as the "Plain Jane Club." All the popular girls at North High were part of a clique. It was an unwritten rule that "Sno-Daze" queens, cheerleaders, and dates for football players had to come from that select group. Although superficially friendly, these self-crowned princesses jealously guarded their position and ganged up on any competition. Renee and the others got the message.

However, when Barbie (affectionately known as "Barbie Doll" among the guys at school) moved next door, Renee started to see that beneath the facade was a very insecure girl. After hearing her pastor's sermon, "Does your neighbor know Jesus?", Renee realized that God wanted her to witness to Barbie. However, Renee had bought the lie that she and her friends were inferior to Barbie and her clique. Even the idea of sharing Christ with Barbie filled her with fear. She felt totally weak and helpless. But she remembered a verse she learned as a child: "Not by might nor by power, but by my Spirit, says the

Lord Almighty" (Zech. 4:6). She knew that all her strength had to come from the Holy Spirit, and she diligently prayed for that power.

Then one day she saw Barbie in the backyard. She knew that this was her opportunity. Although her knees were shaking, Renee called out, "Barbie, I just baked an apple pie. How about coming over for pie *a la mode*?"

"My boyfriend is out of town this weekend and I'm lost without him," Barbie confided. "Fresh apple pie sounds good."

After serving the pie, Renee directed the conversation toward the subject of "purpose in life." Then, trusting the Holy Spirit for her words, she stammered, "Barbie, wouldn't you like to have Jesus in your life?" At that point, the Holy Spirit gave her words to say and totally controlled the conversation. Barbie not only listened respectfully but she confessed her need for God.

You can have many such experiences in your life if, after admitting your weakness and acknowledging your dependence on the Holy Spirit, you take the leap of faith. Jesus told at least two people, "Take up your bed and walk." If the first step hadn't been taken, the miracle wouldn't have occurred. You can keep on singing, "Yes, Jesus loves me . . . I am weak, but He is strong." But unless you decide to walk on the water, to witness to your friend, to believe God to heal your broken heart, or to receive strength to complete the seemingly impossible task, His strength won't ever become yours.

Start the conversation—and let God finish it. Decide to find happiness in God alone, and accept the joy of Jesus. Begin working and watch how God sends unexpected help.

If you want to walk on the water, you've got to get out of the boat—and keep your eyes fixed on Jesus.

MEMORIZE

"Pray also for me, that whenever I open my mouth, words may be given me so that I will fearlessly make known the mystery of the gospel" (Eph. 6:19).

PERSONALIZE

I will pray and ask others to pray for me, so that whenever I say anything, I'll be receiving my words from the Holy Spirit. Only then will I be fearless in telling others the good news of Jesus Christ.

PRAY THE VERSE, APPLYING IT TO YOUR LIFE

Dear God, I give my mouth to you and ask you to tell me what to say. Only you can give me the power to witness boldly and effectively.

RECEIVE STRENGTH FROM JESUS TO WITNESS

After praying about it, make a list of five people you wish to witness to. Like Paul, ask others to pray that words will be given you to fearlessly explain the gospel. Pray for these people every day. Pray for opportunities to share Christ with them. Expect power from Jesus as you confront your fear of the reactions you'll receive.

5 people
- Amy
- Christina
- Kim
- Jen J.
- Jen O.

Don't Call the Fire Department

Don was lead guitarist in the musical group their youth pastor had organized. After a lot of practicing and praying, they went on a week's tour. Monday night the response was tremendous. People loved the music and listened attentively to the testimonies and the preaching. Ten people came forward to accept Jesus into their lives.

But after giving the same program four nights in a row, it became routine. The feeling of inadequacy that had once driven everyone to prayer and complete dependence on the Holy Spirit was subtly replaced with a "the-show-must-go-on-and-we-can-do-it-by-ourselves" attitude. Prayer became more of a ceremony than a time to receive desperately needed help from God. On Friday night, the sound system failed to function properly, Debbie forgot the words to her solo and, worst of all, there was a dryness to their presentation. Praising God had nearly become "old hat." It was like the Holy Spirit power connection had been unplugged.

You need to learn the same lesson as Don and his friends. Your source of strength is the Holy Spirit—not natural ability, experience, or talent. Like an old-fashioned train locomotive that needs fire in its engine to pull the train, you need the power of the Holy Spirit in your spirit. The Bible tells us, "Do not put out the Spirit's fire" (1 Thess. 5:19). In order to obey this verse, you need to ask yourself this question: "What makes a fire go out?"

Without enough fuel a fire will die. The Holy Spirit uses Scripture as the catalyst to bring revelation to your heart. If you don't meditate on the Bible, how can that fire keep burning? If you don't continually claim the strength of the Holy Spirit in prayer, you start running on your own power, and you'll wear yourself out. Because of neglect, so many fail to take advantage of the power of the Holy Spirit within them.

Do you ever pour the cold water of doubt or fear on the flame within your heart? Do you hesitate to let the Holy Spirit be himself in you? Do you get scared when you think of letting the Spirit's supernatural power flood your life? Say *no* to doubt and fear but *yes* to faith.

You can also smother the blaze with the dirt of sin. The Bible declares: "He who conceals his sin does not prosper" (Prov. 28:13). The power of the Holy Spirit was taken away from Samson because he sinned. The same thing will happen to you if you don't confess wrongdoing and receive God's forgiveness.

Winds of trials and difficulty will attempt to extinguish the blaze. But wind can either snuff out a fire or whip it into a fury. Adopt an attitude that says, "Though war break out against me, even then will I be confident" (Ps. 27:3). Then winds of adversity can only fan the flame.

One last thing to remember is that the fire department of public opinion is always ready to fight the fire of the Holy Spirit. Worldly friends and lukewarm Christians will feel uncomfortable around "on-fire fanatics."

Decide to take orders from heavenly headquarters. And whatever you do, don't call the fire department.

MEMORIZE

"For this reason I remind you to fan into flame the gift of God, which is in you through the laying on of my hands. For God did not give up a spirit of timidity, but a spirit of power, of love and of self-discipline" (1 Tim. 1:6–7).

VISUALIZE

PERSONALIZE

I will stir up the spiritual gifts within me. I will remember that God's Spirit inside me drives out fear and gives me power and love and self-discipline.

PRAY THE VERSE, APPLYING IT TO YOUR LIFE

Dear God, thank you for the gifts the Holy Spirit has given me. I promise to exercise these gifts and to permit the Holy Spirit to be himself in me. Lord, I don't accept fear of _____ . I actively receive your strength, your love and your self-discipline.

MEDITATE ON SCRIPTURE

Make a duplicate of this card and take it along with you today. Keep repeating the verse in your mind and decide how it should change your life. Go to sleep thinking about this verse.

Joy: the Power Plant for Christian Living

At least Tami hadn't fallen out of a tenth-story window or boarded the wrong plane—headed for Johannesburg. But that was small comfort. Because she had overslept and missed the chemistry test, she had to take the more difficult makeup test. Although she was starved because she hadn't had time for breakfast, she just couldn't face lunchroom food, so she ate a Jell-O salad and drank a carton of milk. She'd been running on nervous energy for weeks but now she seemed to be operating in the fog of total exhaustion.

The next day at school Tami felt completely drained. Like a robot, she went from room to room, opened her books to pages indicated and handed the homework papers to the person in front of her. When sixth hour ended, Mary asked to have a little talk with her. Not known for tact or her ability to listen to others' opinions, Mary said it all in one sentence. "Tami, you don't dress like a Christian, you don't talk like a Christian, and you don't act like a Christian."

Although Tami knew that most people disregarded everything Mary said, she felt confused and hurt by the statement. *If I'm that bad*, she thought, *maybe even God doesn't love me.* And thinking this made her even more tired and depressed.

Later, Christi noticed that Tami just wasn't the same. "What's the matter?" she asked with concern.

"I don't know," replied Tami. "I'm totally bummed

out and I guess I just don't care anymore. I don't think I can ever be a good Christian."

"I think I know how to help you," Christi comforted. "Have you ever read Nehemiah 8:10? It says: 'The joy of the Lord is your strength.' When you learn how to receive true happiness from God, you'll find that strength and encouragement are included in the package."

Tami thought a minute and realized that Christi had hit the nail on the head. But she had no idea how to regain the joy of the Lord.

If you give yourself a quick spiritual health checkup, you may come up with the same self-diagnosis. And there are some scriptural prescriptions for this disorder.

Jesus taught us something very important. He told us to remain in His love "so that my joy may be in you and that your joy may be complete" (John 15:11). The security of being loved brings happiness to the heart. It's a fact that the true joy of Jesus is the birthright of every believer— and that joy doesn't depend on circumstances. God's joy generates strength just like a hydroelectric power plant. But it can easily become clogged by unbelief, deception, disobedience, or placing attention on boredom and exhaustion rather than on Jesus, the source of joy.

That discouragement and fatigue go together is common knowledge. That's the time to remember that the joy of the Lord is your strength. You not only claim joy but you actively fight for it by expressing praise to God morning, noon, and night. Paul writes to the Philippians: "Rejoice in the Lord always. I will say it again: Rejoice" (Phil. 4:4). We find this principle again in Eph. 5:19–20: "Sing and make music in your heart to the Lord, *always* giving thanks to God"—even if you're tired. These aren't suggestions. They're commands. The joy of Jesus inside you must be expressed or the flowing water that keeps the power plant going will be cut off. By faith you believe that Jesus accomplished His purpose, "that they may have the full measure of my joy within them" (John 17:13). And by faith you obey the command to rejoice in the Lord and give thanks always. Every Christian can sing: "I've got joy like a hydroelectric power plant," but only faith and obedience will keep it in working order.

MEMORIZE

"He who sacrifices thank offerings honors me, and he prepares the way so that I may show him the salvation of God" (Ps. 50:23).

VISUALIZE

PERSONALIZE

When I sacrifice (because sometimes I don't feel like it) to thank and praise God, I not only give God honor but open the way for Him to give me the blessings of my salvation, one of which is strength.

PRAY THE VERSE, APPLYING IT TO YOUR LIFE

Dear God, I praise you and thank you for everything—even _____ (situation you consider unfortunate). I honor you, Lord, and expectantly await your strength and blessing for my life.

TRY THANKSGIVING

Make a list of at least fifty things you can thank God for. Sincerely say thank you to God for each of them. Then continue to praise God for who He is and all He has done.

WEEK 6
DAY 4

Self-Examination

1. Are you trying to be a tin soldier hiding all your weaknesses? _____
   If so, what are you going to do about it? _____
2. What does admitting weakness have to do with being a strong Christian? _____

3. What is the next step after admitting your weaknesses? _____

4. If you are totally weak and exhausted, what two things must you keep in mind? _____

5. To receive God's strength for your weaknesses, what must you do? _____

6. To have spiritual strength, you need the fire of the Holy Spirit within you. What things make the fire go out? _____

7. The _____ of the Lord is your strength.
8. How can you change a woe-and-weakness situation to a walking-on-water experience? _____

9. Did you remember at least once this week that in Jesus you're a winner? _____

If so, how did this make a change in your life? _____

10. Did you willingly accept advice or correction from someone recently? _____
Did you disregard counsel? _____
Explain the effect it had on you. _____

---

1. Personal. 2. It allows God to fill my weakness with His strength. He said, "My power is made perfect in weakness" (2 Cor. 12:9). 3. Receiving God's strength. 4. "Remember, in quietness and trust is your strength." Realize that I must revise my schedule so I can spend time with Him. "Those who hope in the Lord will renew their strength." I must receive strength from God. 5. Like walking on water, I must take the first step by faith. 6. Neglect of Bible reading and prayer, receiving doubt instead of exercising faith, sin, bowing to public opinion, forgetting about God's power when trials come. 7. Joy. 8. By having enough faith to get out of your boat—or rut, or cage, and then keeping your eyes on Jesus and following Him. 9.–10. Personal.

PART 4

In Jesus I Am the Light of the World

You are the light of the world.

Matthew 5:14

Who's Afraid of the Light (and Other Useful Information)

Because God miraculously opened many doors, I was able to teach an elective history course called "Bible and Archeology" in a public high school for several years. Especially when I finished the Old Testament and came to the life of Christ, I was aware of a tremendous spiritual battle. As students from extremely varied backgrounds came face-to-face with the claims of Jesus Christ, the persistent opposition of satanic forces was evident. But after a while I noticed something very interesting.

Whenever there were Christian pupils in my class, it seemed that their very presence dispelled darkness and their influence caused others to accept more truth. I remember one class in which there wasn't a single Christian. It was by far the toughest Bible class I've ever taught. On the other hand, when there were three or four grounded believers taking the course, I found teaching relatively easy. And even a weak, struggling Christian made a noticeable difference.

If I had fully realized what Jesus meant when He said, "You are the light of the world," I would have been able to predict the atmosphere of these classes in advance. Jesus didn't say, "Try to be a little candle burning in the night." He didn't admonish, "After three years of Bible school, you'll be equipped with batteries so you can turn on your flashlight." He said, "You *are* [right now] the light of the world."

Jesus also proclaimed, "I am the light of the world. Whoever follows me will never walk in darkness, but will have the light of life" (John 8:12). Jesus is the *big* light who ignites a flame in the heart of each believer—and unless you intentionally cover it up, it will shine.

Just stop to consider it. You *are* the light of the world. You and all the other Christians have the truth that keeps this planet from complete chaos and disintegration. Receive this truth and walk in confidence. Let your light shine.

Even a small light can be seen for a great distance in the darkness. During World War II, complete blackouts were ordered for entire cities. Even a burning candle could aid an enemy pilot in finding his target. You'll never know how much the light you display will accomplish.

Obviously, you should do everything possible to make your light as effective as possible. But right now concentrate on this: "I have the light of life. I am the light of the world." While others complain that the younger generation is going to the dogs, that the world is more wicked than ever, and that being good is old-fashioned, you guide your life by this fact: "I am the light of the world. Darkness can never hurt light, and I am light. The darker it is, the more noticeable light becomes."

The powers of darkness are afraid of light. And you are the light of the world!

Please Pass the Salt

It was a great sermon, and Sandi was being totally convicted.

"Do everything without complaining or arguing," the pastor read from Phil. 2:14. He continued: "Do you complain about the service in the restaurant, the prices in the stores, and other drivers on the road? Do you murmur about your boss, your teachers, your school assignments and doing homework? Do you find fault with your friends, your parents and relatives? If you do, it's sin. When the Israelites complained about the food in the desert, they all came down with quail poisoning! God punishes murmurers because He hates the sin of complaining."

Sandi decided that her attitude needed a complete overhaul.

After a while, her friend Amanda asked, "What's your secret? How can you have such a positive attitude all the time?"

But then it happened. The geometry teacher used an old test that included problems from the chapter they hadn't studied yet. When he refused to discount the unfair questions, Sandi decided that "do everything without complaining or arguing" couldn't possibly refer to unfair teachers. She started arguing with the teacher and threatened to take the matter to the office. When she got a *C* on the test, she became the self-appointed committee chairperson for processing complaints about Mr. Parallelogram's class. Sandi began to question everything her teacher did. Amanda was shocked, and she lost interest in learning more about Sandi's secret.

Jesus had something to say about Sandi's situation—something you need to know, too. "You are the salt of the earth. But if the salt loses its saltiness, how can it be made salty again? It is no longer good for anything, except to be thrown out and trampled by men" (Matt. 5:13).

Salt preserves, cleanses and brings out flavor. People who obey the Word of God in the power of the Holy Spirit are the salt of the earth. They uphold standards of right and wrong. They spread light and love in an atmosphere of distrust and discouragement. They speak out against wrongdoing and are honest in their dealings. Their very presence changes the choice of vocabulary and the topic of conversation in a group. The way they live convicts others of their sin. Seeing life from Jesus' point of view, they have a zest for living that is contagious. They add extra flavor to life. And if you're close to Jesus, obeying His Word every day, you *are* the salt of the earth.

As long as salt doesn't combine itself with other substances, it maintains its full strength. Continually living in God's will, you *are* salt, and wherever you go, you bring righteousness and light along with you. It isn't an effort. It just happens. But when you dilute God's truth with your reasoning, the newest psychological theory, or public opinion polls, you lose your saltiness. Compromising with the world discredits your testimony. If there is any salt in your life that has lost its flavor, throw it all out and start over with Jesus. Anything that's partially Christian and partially of the world is fit only for the garbage. Half and half just doesn't make it.

But if you stay salty, you're a terribly important person. Potatoes or planets without salt are worthless. And remember one thing. Salt isn't usually noticed—only its absence is worthy of mention. Live so that when you graduate, or change jobs, or move to another city people will in their own way say, "Please pass the salt"—"I sure miss her"—"She was always so cheerful"—"One could never find a more honest and reliable employee"—"He's the one who witnessed to me before I became a Christian."

MEMORIZE

"But thanks be to God, who always leads us in triumphal procession in Christ and through us spreads everywhere the fragrance of the knowledge of him" (2 Cor. 2:14).

VISUALIZE

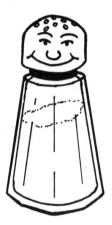

PERSONALIZE

I will thank God because in Christ I'm always part of the victory parade. Jesus also uses me to display the sweet fragrance of the knowledge of God contrasted with the decaying odor of selfishness, greed and rebellion.

PRAY THE VERSE, APPLYING IT TO YOUR LIFE

Thank you, God, that as I follow close to Jesus, I'm always in the company of winners even if _____ (something that appears as though it might defeat you). Thank you that because Jesus lives in me, He uses me to spread the sweetness of knowing Him everywhere I go.

GET A FRESH SUPPLY OF "SALT OF THE EARTH"

Ask Jesus where you've compromised or used your own salt substitute. Determine to stay salty by keeping close to God, "who always leads us in a triumphal procession in Christ and through us spreads everywhere the fragrance of the knowledge of him."

Indestructible Light Meets Big Bad Bluff

Phil and Bart had been neighbors since kindergarten. They had gone through grade school and junior high together. Tenth-graders and still good friends, they were in the same biology class. Phil realized one day, after he had rededicated his life to Christ, that he had never really witnessed to Bart. He could wake up in heaven someday and find Bart missing! He began to pray for Bart and waited for a good opportunity to speak to him. When Bart's grandfather died, Phil told Bart that all of us had to prepare for death and if he accepted Jesus as his Savior, he could be sure of heaven. Phil was totally shocked at Bart's response: "Man is a product of the evolutionary process," he lectured. "We all return to the earth to become part of nature. Heaven and other myths are for weaklings who can't face the world as it is. If you want to keep my friendship, preach to someone else."

Feeling he had failed in his attempt to witness to Bart, Phil opened his Bible to read something before going to bed. John 1:5 could just as well have been printed in neon light: "The light shines in the darkness, but the darkness has not understood it."

Suddenly Phil saw things more clearly. It isn't necessarily the fault of the light when it is rejected. Some people find light very uncomfortable. Eyes that have been in darkness for a long time hurt when they are exposed to bright light. Actions that seem perfectly okay when the lights are low somehow seem less respectable under the spotlight. Darkness hides dirt, cockroaches and crime. There are many places where light just isn't welcome.

As a lit-up Christian in a dark world, you need to be able to cope with the fact that some people love darkness rather than light. Righteousness can be most unpopular with the crowd. But you need to be convinced that the world needs light whether or not it wants it. You—because Jesus lives in you—are the signpost that points the way to heaven, the example of right living, and the catalyst for positive change. Don't get discouraged. Decide to be the best light you can be. Shine, even when those around you seek shadow shelters. Get wisdom from God so you know when your witness should be verbal and when it should be silent. But never give up.

And don't forget that you never have to be afraid of the dark. John 1:5 is also translated: "The light shines in the darkness, but the darkness has not overcome it." Darkness does not understand light or appreciate it, but can do nothing to extinguish it. The light that is literally from out of this world—the light that Jesus imparts to each Christian—can't be unplugged, or smashed, or smothered. It can only be dimmed or turned off from an inside switch.

Every day there'll be a battle between indestructible light and the big bad bluff of darkness. But like the light of the most distant stars, the life of Jesus inside you will keep shining no matter how much darkness it must shine through.

INDESTRUCTIBLE LIGHT

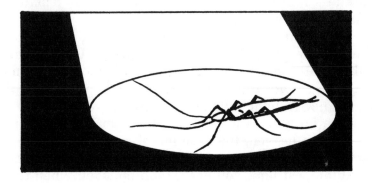

MEMORIZE

"This is the verdict: Light has come into the world, but men loved darkness instead of light because their deeds were evil" (John 3:19).

PERSONALIZE

Jesus is the light. If I ever get entangled with sin, I feel uncomfortable around Him. Jesus gives His light to me. As I shine for Him, I must learn that many people who enjoy sinning will reject me, but they can't do anything to ruin my light.

PRAY THE VERSE, APPLYING IT TO YOUR LIFE

Dear God, thank you for sending Jesus, the light of the world. Thank you for putting that light in me. Although _____ (problem you face because of your Christian testimony), I will not become discouraged. I will remember that some people like the darkness and hate the light.

ADOPT A "LET-YOUR-LIGHT-SHINE" MENTALITY

List all the negative things that could possibly happen to you if you constantly shared your faith. After each one write: "The light shines in the darkness, but the darkness has not overcome it" and "Men loved darkness instead of light because their deeds were evil." Just remember that no one can put out your light and that you are not a failure even if people don't accept your message. Let Jesus teach you what it means to be the light of the world.

Full Moons? Eclipses? and Son Reflectors

Mitsy accepted Christ as her Savior in March. Because of the power of the Holy Spirit in her life, she stopped taking drugs and her life changed drastically. She just couldn't get enough of the Bible, and her face shone as she told others about Jesus. During the summer she got a lot of fellowship, and her week at Bible camp proved to be a mountaintop experience. She felt ready to face the world.

What she didn't realize was that Christians don't run on stored-up energy. Since she was starting her senior year, she got a job to save money for college and became so busy that she hardly had time for Bible study and prayer. When Doug invited her to homecoming, she accepted, even though she knew he wasn't a Christian. Soon dates with him devoured her church time. She began to look worn out. The light in her eyes was gone. She was much too far from the Son to reflect His light.

Maybe Mitsy's experience is like yours. Perhaps you wonder why you have no real desire to witness. You may be saying to yourself, "I feel more like a 15-watt bulb than like the light of the world." Then you need to understand the principle behind your being the light of the world and to line your life up with this truth.

None of the light you diffuse comes from you. Christians are like little moons reflecting the light of Jesus.

Whether you're a quarter moon or a full moon depends on how much of your life you expose to that Light. Have you given your mouth to Jesus to be used to speak His words? Or have you become a half moon by deciding that you'll witness only with your life. Is there an area—your friendships and dates, your passion for sports, your determination to buy whatever you wish—that has not been surrendered to Jesus and therefore remains darkened? Are there pockets of selfishness, pride and an inability to take correction that spread a haze over the light you received from Jesus?

It's also possible to experience an eclipse. If the earth's shadow covers the moon, it cannot reflect the sun's light. Are you letting something or someone cast a shadow over your life so that the light of Jesus can't get through?

Although it is good to receive training in evangelism, lack of know-how is never the fundamental problem that keeps people from sharing their faith. It's that they are experiencing their own eclipses—something is blocking the light of the Son. Decide that eclipses are not for you. Fall in love with Jesus. Cultivate an intimacy with Him that assures that you, as a little light of the world, will mirror the total glory of Jesus who came to dispel darkness.

It's so important that you stay close to Him, because Jesus went back to heaven and left you and the other Son reflectors in charge of "Operation Light Up the World."

MEMORIZE

"You, O Lord, keep my lamp burning; my God turns my darkness into light" (Ps. 18:28).

VISUALIZE

PERSONALIZE

I get all the light in my life from Jesus. I must stay very close to Him so I can reflect His light. I will turn all the dark areas in my life toward Jesus so He can saturate me with His light.

PRAY THE VERSE, APPLYING IT TO YOUR LIFE

Dear God, I ask you to give me light today so I can share it with others. You know that _____ (dark area in your life) isn't a good testimony. I confess my sin and ask you to light up this dark spot.

MEDITATE ON SCRIPTURE

Take this verse with you today. Think about it, pray it, and let it change your life. Go to sleep with the words of this verse running through your mind.

Join the Son Worshipers

Jenifer had gone to youth group activities for over six months. Dreadfully lonely, she liked the fact that the others accepted her and cared for her. Confused by the influence of a lot of false doctrine, she still hadn't been able to accept the fact that she was a sinner and needed salvation. When Jerry, a 25-year-old gas station attendant started to ask her out, she enjoyed being the center of his attention. One day, as she was telling him how difficult her home situation was, he came up with a solution: "Why don't you move in with me?"

When she mentioned the possibility to the girls at church, they all told her the same thing. But she noticed a difference in the way they expressed biblical truth. Char had responded fearfully, "Jenifer, you can't do that! You'll ruin your whole life. If you disobey God, there's no hope for you." Darlene's words were edged with pride: "You should know better than that, Jenifer. How can you even consider a lifestyle that's for prostitutes and atheists? I couldn't even think of sinning like that!" Naomi stuttered and stammered. "I know everybody's doing it. I'm sure that what I'm going to say sounds old-fashioned. You might think I'm a stick-in-the-mud, but it's wrong to sleep with your boyfriend."

However, Donna was able to give it to her straight, with confidence on her face and love in her voice. "Jenifer, I know it's a big temptation right now, but sinning against God's law never makes anything better. It will only get you into bigger trouble later on. But my advice isn't that important. Let's look at what God has to say. Here it is in 1 Thess. 4:3: 'It is God's will that you should be holy; that you should avoid sexual immorality.' "

All four girls were being the light of the world in the sense that they were giving out right information which could push back darkness and deception. But only Donna had learned the secret of Ps. 34:5: "Those who look to him are radiant; their faces are never covered with shame." Don't be the light that flickers from fear. Don't blind others with power surges of pride. Always keep your eyes on Him. Be a broadcaster of His truth only. Don't mix it with your emotions or your own point of view. Don't dilute it with the darkness around you. Reflect only what you receive from Jesus.

Probably the most difficult lesson to learn is that, because the light we reflect comes directly from Jesus, neither the water of discouragement nor the winds of trial, nor the suffocation of criticism need affect your Son reflector. Although the devil tries to tell you that you're a little candle that can be snuffed out at any time, the truth is that you are a Son reflector, made of supernatural substance which God put into your spirit when you were born again. Satan's only hope is to get you off balance enough so that you step out of the direct Son-light.

Stop worrying about your every word and your every action. Forget about the odds against you and the difficulties all around. Become a devoted Son Worshiper whose only concern is being in the right position so you can reflect all of His light all of the time.

JOIN THE SON WORSHIPERS

MEMORIZE

"For God, who said, 'Let light shine out of darkness,' made his light shine in our hearts to give us the light of the knowledge of the glory of God in the face of Christ" (2 Cor. 4:6).

PERSONALIZE

God who created light to break through darkness had put that light in my heart. As I look straight into the face of Jesus, His glory becomes mine. If I maintain this close relationship with Jesus, I'll automatically be a good Son reflector.

PRAY THE VERSE, APPLYING IT TO YOUR LIFE

Dear God, thanks for creating light. Thanks for putting your light in my heart. Thanks for showing me that I can reflect your light only as I keep looking at Jesus. Forgive me for concentrating on _____ (problem or fear) instead of looking at the radiant face of Jesus.

LINE YOUR LIFE UP WITH JESUS

Determine to do everything necessary to gain the approval of Jesus. Make Jesus the love of your life. Forget about everything else and get so close to Him that you reflect His light.

Speeding Tickets, Craving Chocolate, and Being the Light of the World

Mitch just sat there and said nothing. The biology teacher had asked for volunteers for a debate between creationists and evolutionists. Three people volunteered to debate on the side of evolution. Only Brenda said she wanted to represent the creationist point of view. Mitch was a Christian and he believed that the Genesis account of how God created the world was totally correct. It's just that he was afraid of what the other kids would think of him.

Later in the day, a poem they were studying in English class evoked a discussion on belief in life after death. As students were giving different opinions, Mitch knew that this was a perfect opportunity to witness to his class, but paralyzed by fear, he kept silent. Even though he went home feeling guilty, he knew that tomorrow would be no different.

Have you ever been in Mitch's situation? Most people would have to answer, "Yes." Thinking seriously about it, you'd have to admit that it's totally illogical for the light of the world to refuse to shine. Jesus said it this way: "No one lights a lamp and puts it in a place where it is hidden" (Luke 11:33). Although we know that concealing light from people stumbling through the darkness makes no sense, we need to examine the cause in order to come up with the cure.

I once heard a speaker make this comment, "The answer to every how question in the Christian life is the Holy Spirit." It is 100 percent true that as you stay ever so close to Jesus, you automatically reflect His light. But you will ask, "How do I do that?" And the answer to your question is, "By the power of the Holy Spirit." The Holy Spirit is the infallible computer on the inside of you that tells you when you're straying away from Jesus, that gives you power to stand up for Jesus in a hostile crowd, and tells you what to say and how to say it when opportunities to witness arise. Until you give the Holy Spirit free rein to manifest himself any way He wishes in your life, your Christian witness will be weak and anemic.

In 1 Thess. 5:19 we read, "Do not put out the Spirit's fire." Resisting what the Holy Spirit wants to do through you dims your light. The Holy Spirit not only tells us when and how to speak, but shows us that at times it is much better to say nothing. The whole key to verbal witnessing is found in Matt. 10:19–20. "Do not worry about what to say or how to say it. At that time you will be given what to say, for it will not be you speaking, but the Spirit of your Father speaking through you." If Christians truly put this verse into practice, both the "tongue-tied, red-faced, I'm-too-shy-to-witness" excuse-givers and the "blast-forth-the-recorded-message" mechanical parrots would disappear from the face of the earth.

But many are so busy condemning these extremes that they never take time to listen to the Holy Spirit within. Determine to learn from the Holy Spirit how to stay close to Jesus and to let your light shine. Only the Holy Spirit can keep you from hiding your light or using a spotlight that blinds instead of illumines. And if you ever wonder, "How can I—the person who has trouble loving my little brother, who likes to break the speed limit, and who has to pass Fanny Farmer on the other side of the street to keep from OD-ing on chocolate—ever be the light of the world?" The answer is this: "Not by might nor by power but by my Spirit, says the Lord Almighty" (Zech. 4:6).

MEMORIZE

"Let your light shine before men, that they may see your good deeds and praise your Father in heaven" (Matt. 5:16).

VISUALIZE

PERSONALIZE

I really am the light of the world and my light will shine if I let it. People need to see goodness in me that will bring honor to God and draw people to Him.

PRAY THE VERSE, APPLYING IT TO YOUR LIFE

Dear God, thank you for the command to let my light shine. I determine now to let the Holy Spirit have His way in my life so this will happen. (Don't pray unless you mean it!) You know I'm having trouble with _____ (something you should do). Help me change this so people will see the quality of my life and praise God because of me.

LET THE HOLY SPIRIT BE HIMSELF IN YOU

Take your foot off the brakes and let the Holy Spirit be himself in you. Ask God to reveal the fears and the reservations that dim your light. Give these things over to God.

Do Yourself a Favor

For the first time in her life, Michelle was sitting in the principal's office. And she was there for talking back to a teacher—something she never dreamed she could have been guilty of. She had always been the model student and had just been elected to the National Honor Society. Although she wasn't very interested in sports, she had always done her best in Phys Ed class. She had to admit, though, that Miss Barnett tried her patience to the limit.

Naturally compassionate and sympathetic, Michelle always took the part of the underdog. When Miss Barnett directed her sarcasm toward her and others who lacked athletic ability, Michelle steamed and seethed on the inside. That day Miss Barnett chose to pick on Angela, who was timid, pathetically scatter-brained, and definitely not intellectually gifted.

Before handing back the exams, Miss Barnett had commented, "Do any of you ever study? Here's a test that reads, 'A full count is when a batter has three balls and four strikes.' " Everybody laughed as she handed Angela her test. At this Michelle boiled over.

She stood up and shouted: "And do you ever care about your students? All you do is put people down and make fun of them. This is the worst class I've ever been in, and you're the worst teacher I've ever had." Michelle

116

had even surprised herself. She had no idea there was that much bitterness and animosity inside her.

For this she was now sitting in the principal's office. And his first words to her shocked her: "I thought you were a Christian. I never expected to see *you* here."

Michelle wondered how the principal had found out she was a Christian. And at that moment she realized that the scope of her testimony was much broader than she had ever imagined. What she did and said really mattered, and she knew she needed to walk closer to Jesus so she could reflect much more of His light.

The Bible tells us, "For you were once darkness, but now you are light in the Lord. Live as children of light (for the fruit of the light consists in all goodness, righteousness and truth) and find out what pleases the Lord" (Eph. 5:8–10). You need to be conscious of the fact that the beams of your light reach a lot farther than you once thought. When you stray away from Jesus, people you don't even know will suffer because the lights went out.

Although you need to be aware of the importance of consistently letting your light shine, you can't let it become a burden. If you, like Michelle, blow it completely on occasion, it is important to confess and forsake your sin immediately. Determine not to let the shadows of condemnation block the light of Jesus. Just get closer to Jesus than ever before so you can reflect more light. If you forget about yourself and become completely taken up with praising, loving and serving Jesus, your light can't help but shine.

There's an old song that says, "Everybody loves a lover." And it's basically true, because the person in love usually has a shining countenance, a contagious happiness and some love left over for others. When you fall in love with Jesus so that all you want is to be near Him, you'll become more and more like Him, brightening up the darkness wherever you go.

Do yourself and everyone else a favor. Enjoy receiving—and automatically giving—the light and love of Jesus.

VISUALIZE BRIGHTENING UP YOUR WORLD

MEMORIZE

"Be imitators of God, therefore, as dearly loved children and live a life of love, just as Christ loved us and gave himself up for us as a fragrant offering and sacrifice to God" (Eph. 5:1–2).

PERSONALIZE

I know that if I'm going to imitate God, I must spend a lot of time receiving from Him. If I receive His love and all the things He died to give me, I'll be equipped to live a life of love—just like Jesus.

PRAY THE VERSE, APPLYING IT TO YOUR LIFE

Dear God, thank you for being my perfect role model. I aim to spend so much time with you that I become like you. Thank you for Jesus' love for me. I receive that love so I can give it to others.

MEDITATE ON SCRIPTURE

Take this verse with you today. Study it at every opportunity. Let it change you and make you more like Jesus. Think about it as you go to sleep tonight.

Enjoying the Son Light, Even on Cloudy Days

Linda sat there stunned. How could it be true? Her father had just announced that he was leaving and moving in with his secretary. Her mother was sobbing in the living room while her older brother tried to comfort her. Her sister was screaming at her father, but Linda just sat there paralyzed. Anger welled up within her. Where was God? How could He allow such a thing to happen in her family? How could her father violate the standards he had always taught his own children?

For weeks Linda operated in a fog. She went to church only out of habit. Her prayers seemed to bounce back at her, and she couldn't concentrate when she tried to read the Bible. She felt guilty for being a bad testimony, but it seemed as if the light had disappeared from her life. Desperate, she decided she must do something—anything. She volunteered to teach a Sunday school class, joined the choir, and went to the beach witnessing. But her heart wasn't in it. She yelled at the Sunday school kids, cried when the choir director tried to correct her, and ended up agreeing with the girl who said she'd believe in God when He changed some circumstances in her life.

Finally, she poured her heart out to Beth, the one friend she really felt she could trust. Beth listened carefully and then said, "There's a couple verses in Isaiah that you need to get acquainted with: 'Who among you fears the Lord and obeys the word of his servant? Let him who walks in the dark, who has no light, trust in the name of the Lord and rely on his God. But now, all you who light fires and provide yourselves with flaming torches, go, walk in the light of your fires and of the torches you have set ablaze. This you shall receive from my hand; you will lie down in torment' (Isa. 50:10–11).

"Linda," Beth continued, "as a Christian you're to mirror the light of Jesus. But sometimes the whole sky appears cloudy and you feel like you can't find any light to reflect. Instead of just trusting that God is there and hanging on in faith waiting for Him to come to the rescue, the human reaction is to panic.

"We hurriedly erect a good front, we try to repair the damage with tools that weren't made for the job, or we become so busy we have no time to think. We forget that back of the clouds, the Son is still shining, that God's Word is still true, and that God's love is constant no matter how we feel.

"The devil tries to make you feel guilty about a cloud that wasn't your fault," she continued. "He tries to tell you that feeling as though you are walking in darkness is wrong. That's not true. However, the fires we light to try to scare away the darkness get us into deep trouble because they're all the result of one underlying sin—lack of faith. The Bible says: 'Let him who walks in the dark . . . trust in the name of the Lord.' You need to throw yourself into the arms of Jesus and let Him give you light. Put your confidence in Him.

"Another thing, Linda," Beth counseled, "is to realize that light does come through clouds. It's not pitch black on a cloudy day—you can even get sunburn. There've been times when I've been really down but God would still send someone to me for spiritual help. I'd tell Him, 'You'll have to do it all. I feel like I have nothing to give.' And His light has shown through me even when I thought I was walking in darkness."

Clouds of tragedy, stress, and heartbreak can't eradicate the light of the Son. You need to learn that clouds can't keep you from being a Son reflector. Only the panic that makes you light your own fires instead of trusting God can place you in a position where you receive nothing from the Light of the World.

When things fall apart, remember that you can keep on enjoying the Son-light, even on cloudy days.

MEMORIZE

"Light is shed upon the righteous and joy on the upright in heart" (Ps. 97:11).

VISUALIZE

PERSONALIZE

I believe that light is shed on me—even when I see nothing but clouds and blackness. I believe that joy is God's gift to me when my heart is right with God.

PRAY THE VERSE, APPLYING IT TO YOUR LIFE

Dear God, thank you that your light is shining on me even when I feel surrounded by darkness and I'm confused about _____ . Thank you that you have joy for me when I obey you. I claim that joy in spite of feeling depressed about _____ .

BELIEVE THAT GOD IS HANDING OUT LIGHT AND JOY

By faith, get in line with the expectation that He's got plenty left for you—even if discouragement decided to go to school with you today.

Self-Examination

1. Even if the world gets worse, you are the _____·
   of the world which shines even brighter in utter
   blackness. _____ can never hurt light.
2. It is always my fault if I witness to somebody and they
   reject the message of Christ.   T F
3. Many people love darkness rather than light and will
   reject the message of Christ no matter how it is
   presented.   T F
4. If I am not witnessing, it's because
   _____ a. I've never had enough training.
   _____ b. I'm shy.
   _____ c. I'm not close enough to the Son to reflect His
            light.
   _____ d. My "mission field" is just too tough for me.

5. When you feel like you're walking in darkness
   _____ a. Whistle a happy tune.
   _____ b. Walk by pure faith, remembering that the
            clouds aren't your fault—(unless, of course,
            you've sinned, in which case you must con-
            fess and forsake wrongdoing). Realize that
            the Son is there behind the clouds shining on
            you.
   _____ c. Panic.
   _____ d. Become so busy you don't have time to think.

6. How can a fallible person like you really be the light of the world?_____

7. How can you be fully aware of the scope of your testimony without feeling like you're under a heavy burden?_____

8. What if you really want to be a good testimony but you blow it completely?_____

9. What are two steps to spiritual strength?_____

10. God always leads me in triumphal procession in Christ, but I must _____

PART 5

In Jesus I Am Competent

But our competence comes from God.
He has made us competent as
ministers of a new covenant.

2 Corinthians 3:5–6

The Rise and Fall of "Superman Christian"

Eric sat in the dugout with his teammates, unable to believe his ears. The coach was benching him for two weeks.

"The guy must have rocks in his head!" thought Eric. "With a batting average of .503, nearly as many RBI's as the rest of the team combined, and a perfect fielding record, I'm the star of the team." He tuned in to the coach's speech: "We all know that Eric Thompson is the most talented player to come through Park High in years. It's just that this is a team—not a one-man show. I put Eric in center field to play that position only. Because he's all over the outfield and tries to make spectacular catches in the second baseman's territory, you guys don't function as a team.

"Besides, his constant coaching and criticism of the

others has ruined the self-confidence of more than one player. Learning that the world doesn't revolve around one person is an important lesson that I want to teach all of you. Eric, you're not playing until you learn that you're judged on teamwork, not on individual performance."

Have you ever tried to be the star on God's team? The problem that so many Christians have in feeling confident and competent stems from a wrong idea of what's expected of them. You were created by God with certain gifts and abilities to function in the body of Christ. God purposely made you unable to do everything so you'd have to work with other Christians and depend on them. There are to be no one-man shows in Christianity. The Bible says, "But in fact God has arranged the parts of the body, every one of them, just as he wanted them to be. The eye cannot say to the hand, 'I don't need you,' and the head cannot say to the feet, 'I don't need you!' " (1 Cor. 12:18–21).

The idea of the well-rounded person who can do everything equally well came to the world from non-biblical sources such as the Renaissance man, and from ancient mythology with characters like Ulysses, the man who was never at a loss. If man is the "measure of all things" and there is no God who has a great plan for His world, why not attempt to outdo every other human? However, if an omnipotent God runs the universe and has ordained that you be part of His perfect plan, such an idea seems ridiculous. Being a solo when you're meant to be part of an orchestra can get you into trouble.

As a Christian, you are dependent on God for your sense of competence, and you're part of a team. There are many things God does not expect you to be able to do. Eyes should not try to be hands, and feet should not feel discouraged because they're not heads. The Bible states: "[God] has made us competent as ministers of a new covenant" (2 Cor. 3:6). In other words, God will give you the power to be or do anything that is necessary to communicate the new life Jesus offers to the world—and that may not require bowling 250, walking like a fashion model, getting straight *A's*, or being voted Personality Plus by the senior class.

When you decide you must be superman or bionic woman, you feel incompetent because you're judging yourself by the wrong standard. Pray and ask God what He has called you to do. Rely on the power of the Holy Spirit to do those things well. Believe that God will equip you for the work He wants you to do—but don't expect to excel in every area. Too many have already tried to be one-man shows and have failed. Don't join the casualty list. Don't aspire to be a superman Christian, or you'll be sure to fall.

Competence and a Box Marked Instant Pudding

Tim looked at his guitar and considered throwing it out the window. He was certain he never wanted to play it again—especially in front of the youth group.

He had been thrilled with the opportunity to join those who led the praise and worship time. But because he hadn't practiced enough and didn't know all the songs, he repeatedly messed up. Finally realizing that he had played the entire refrain in the wrong key and too flustered to even think straight, he left the platform and sat down. He was sure that everyone noticed, especially Amber, the girl he most wanted to impress.

Tim wanted more than anything else to use his talent for God and knew it was God's will for him to play in the music group. However, his confidence was gone. He didn't ever want to make such a fool of himself again.

Feelings of incompetence plague everybody at times. Two things are important to learn:

First, when you fail, don't look inside, or beat yourself over the head for having done a bad job. Ability to do something well comes from God. If you're certain God wants you to do it, you have the right to trust God for the capacity to do a good job. "Such confidence as this is ours through Christ before God. Not that we are competent to claim anything for ourselves, but our competence comes from God" (2 Cor. 3:4–6).

Second, God chooses to work in us through a process that requires our cooperation. Although God is capable of any miracle, I've never heard of Him enabling someone to play the piano without a minute's practice, to glide effortlessly down the steepest slope the first time on skis, or to make a gorgeous gown as a beginning seamstress.

Paul's prayer for the Philippians indicates that the need to learn and slowly increase in competence is not limited to abilities in the physical realm. He writes: "And this is my prayer: that your love may abound more and more in knowledge and depth of insight, so that you may be able to discern what is best" (Phil. 1:9–10). People lose it because either they have no faith that competence comes from God or they expect Him to hand it down on a silver platter without their cooperating in faith. Even Jesus, when He took on humanity, was subject to "people principles." He was fully God and He never sinned, but "Jesus grew in wisdom" (Luke 2:52). He didn't preach sermons when He was six months old, and He never appeared in Jerusalem, Jericho and Nazareth at the same time. Accept the limitations of being human, but don't confuse them with lack of faith or use them as excuses for not following God.

God does promise us competence to do what He has called us to do. We can claim it from Him. It's just that it doesn't come prepackaged from heaven in a box marked "Instant Pudding" with an additional bottle of he-man pills for special occasions.

HOW GOD DOESN'T WORK

MEMORIZE

"Being confident of this, that he who began a good work in you will carry it on to completion until the day of Christ Jesus" (Phil. 1:6).

PERSONALIZE

I'm confident, because I know Jesus has begun a good work in me. He will keep on remaking my life until He comes back again. I don't have to be discouraged about _____ because Jesus hasn't given up on me.

PRAY THE VERSE, APPLYING IT TO YOUR LIFE

Dear God, thanks for the fact that I have confidence in you and not in myself. Thank you that you don't leave your products half finished. I ask you to help me with _____ (problems in the area of confidence), and I know you will because you promised.

COOPERATE WITH GOD TO GAIN COMPETENCE

Confess to God impatience and attempts to defy "people principles." Thank Him that He has begun a good work in you and yield yourself to His process of making you competent as His ambassador.

Turn on the Faucet—Full Blast

Marcy broke into tears. To her, life was a pressure-cooker. Existence resembled one of those nightmares in which a person becomes worn out trying to reach the top of the mountain, never making any progress. Only she never woke up to discover it was just a bad dream.

She knew she was supposed to love her enemies, witness to those who don't know Jesus, do her best at all times, and be respectful and obedient to all authorities. Struggling to live up to her Christian standards, she felt like a failure. So many non-Christians she knew seemed so happy-go-lucky that at times she even envied them.

There is a way out of this kind of dilemma. If you attempt to live up to the ideals of Jesus in your own strength, you can feel much less competent than a non-Christian who chooses to live by some human yardstick. (People who don't know Jesus often assume that it's perfectly legitimate to hate those who mistreat them, to get by as easily as possible and to make life difficult for teachers and parents.)

The answer to the problem is the power of the Holy Spirit. " 'Not by might, nor by power, but by my Spirit,' says the Lord Almighty" (Zech. 4:6). If you try to live a supernatural life in human strength, failure is inevitable.

The Holy Spirit in you must live the Christian life.

The Holy Spirit comes to make His home in you when you are "born again"—that miracle which occurs when you invite Jesus to take over your whole life. In fact, the Bible states, "And if anyone does not have the Spirit of Christ, he does not belong to Christ" (Rom. 8:9). After conversion, the question isn't "How much of the Holy Spirit do you have?" It's "How much of *you* does the Holy Spirit possess?"

The Bible teaches that you are to be filled, empowered and permeated with the Holy Spirit. It's a command: "Be filled with the Spirit" (Eph. 5:18). Let the Holy Spirit be himself in you. Search the Scriptures to discover what the Holy Spirit wants to accomplish in your life. Ask God to remove your fear. Surrender your rights to direct your own life. Step out of that box you've been living in and expect new and miraculous workings of the Holy Spirit in *your* life. Receive all the supernatural power, the fruit of the Spirit, and every spiritual gift He has for you.

God didn't intend for you to be an "under-the-pile" Christian like Marcy. His plan is not to lower biblical standards so we won't sense failure, but for us to live the Christian life by the supernatural power of the Holy Spirit. Find a concordance. Look up every reference that tells you about the Holy Spirit. Ask God to give you understanding as you apply these verses to *your* life.

Jesus made a promise: " 'Whoever believes in me as the Scripture has said, streams of living water will flow from within him' " (John 7:38). The water system has already been installed and some of that life-changing liquid is already dripping out. You need to turn on the faucet—full blast—and live in victory as the Holy Spirit flows through you.

MEMORIZE

"[He] is able to do immeasurably more than all we ask or imagine, according to his power that is at work within us" (Eph. 3:20).

VISUALIZE

PERSONALIZE

God is able to do so much more than I can even imagine or ask Him for through the power of His Holy Spirit who lives in me. That means there is power for overcoming _____ (big problem for you).

PRAY THE VERSE, APPLYING IT TO YOUR LIFE

Thank you, God, for giving me the power of the Holy Spirit to work inside me. Thank you that His power is greater than anything I can comprehend. I depend on His power to be victorious in _____ (hard situation).

REPAIR THOSE FAULTY CONNECTIONS

It's really true that Jesus within us can do "immeasurably more than all we ask or imagine." But when we react to situations with our patterns of panic or anger or frustration, we break the connection and cut off the power. Prayerfully ask God what reaction patterns you must break so His power in you can handle your problems.

Give Jesus More Than a Piece of Your Mind

Kevin wished he could wake up and recover from the nightmare. But he was living it out in real life—and he still had to play the second half of the game. As a well-trained athlete who was voted most valuable player by the Jefferson High basketball team in his junior year, Kevin knew that in sports concentration is everything. Tonight, however, he had lost it completely.

Not only had Amy broken up with him, but she had decided to wear a red sweater and sit with her new boyfriend in the front row. To top it off, the fans from Lakeview were making a concentrated effort to heckle him. Self-conscious about his nose, he could hear them chanting, "Pinocchio, Pinocchio, No, No, No." He'd missed six freethrows in a row, had fumbled the ball, and had scored only two points. And he didn't really think he'd meet any nurses on the way to the locker room offering injections of confidence.

As a Christian, you know that you can join Isaiah in telling God, "You will keep in perfect peace him whose mind is steadfast, because he trusts in you" (Isa. 26:3). You're convinced that as long as you keep your eyes on Jesus and not on the waves, you can join Peter in walking with certainty through some pretty tough situations. However, like Kevin, the crises of confidence in your life stem from losing concentration—not fixing your attention totally on Jesus.

Because the devil so cleverly arranges circumstances and uses our weaknesses to undermine us, every honest Christian must admit to the type of defeat Kevin experienced on the basketball court. Maybe you sang your solo entirely wrapped up in what other people were thinking of you instead of singing to offer praise to God. Because the opinion of Jesus was not your only concern, you were devastated when the friend you tried to witness to made fun of you. Perhaps you fell apart when you saw that big red *C* on your chemistry test, because your standards for yourself are more important to you than those Jesus has for you.

Self-consciousness, fear of what others will think, and slavery to the expectations of those around you are chains that we must permit God to break. Then we can receive the sense of confidence and competence God wants to give us.

Don't impose on yourself standards that are not of God. Live by God's expectations—not yours or those of others. Getting rid of unreasonable goals will take off a lot of unneeded pressure. Next, admit that the reason you went through the Kevin-like nightmare was because your eyes were not on Jesus. Confess it as sin and forget it—purposing in your heart not to let it happen again. Finally, practice keeping your thoughts on Jesus by meditating on Scripture. When your mind wants to wander into daydreaming or rehashing circumstances, firmly bring it back to thinking about Him.

That Jesus can fill one's thoughts completely was demonstrated to me in a rather humorous way. As a public-school teacher, I periodically checked the desks in my classroom to wash off objectionable writing. When I came to one desk, I smiled. The student had penciled, "Jesus loves Martha,"[1] "Jesus," "Jesus and Martha."

What's on *your* mind? Is it Jesus? Give Jesus more than a piece of your mind.

---

[1]Name has been changed.

LIVING BY WRONG STANDARDS?

MEMORIZE

"For the Lord will be your confidence and will keep your foot from being snared" (Prov. 3:26).

PERSONALIZE

God has promised to be my confidence. My part is to fix my eyes on Him. He has promised to keep me from tripping. I just need to watch where He is going.

PRAY THE VERSE, APPLYING IT TO YOUR LIFE

Dear God, thank you for being my confidence when _____ (problem area). Thank you that you'll keep me from stumbling when

_____ .

MEDITATE ON SCRIPTURE

Take this verse with you today. Think about it and what it can mean in your life. Go to sleep meditating on this verse.

Have You Won Any Beauty Contests Recently?

Kelly just stared into space and tried to blink away the tears that were filling her eyes. After running downstairs to answer her telephone call, she had lingered in the hallway, eaves-dropping on the conversation between her mother and a friend who was visiting from New York. Her mother's friend was bragging about her daughter: "Teri gets straight *A*'s, has received a scholarship to the most prestigious college in the East, plays violin solos with the symphony, has earned several awards in figure-skating competition, and has won two beauty contests."

"Well," her mother had replied, "I guess Kelly is just Kelly. She doesn't excel in anything—but she's a good kid."

Like soldiers—marching, marching, marching, never breaking rank—thoughts invaded Kelly's mind: "Why do I have to be just average in everything? What's wrong with me? Why can't I be special? I'm just incompetent, that's all." In fact, she had always had problems feeling confident—especially in new situations.

Kelly is not alone. There are many people who share her feelings. Perhaps you're one of them. If so, the book of Colossians has something to say to you. "See to it that no one takes you captive through hollow and deceptive philosophy, which depends on human tradition and the basic principles of this world rather than Christ . . . And you have been given fullness in Christ, who is the head over every power and authority" (Col. 2:8, 10). The King James Version of the Bible states it this way, "And ye are complete in him." The RSV translates it, "You have come to fullness of life in him."

Getting down to the nitty-gritty, the Bible says you are complete and have abundant life in Christ. You can choose to believe it and receive that fullness from Jesus, or you can endlessly compare yourself with unusually talented or good-looking people. You can take what God says about you at face value or you can let someone else's standards destroy your sense of competence.

If you have Jesus you have everything—and so much of what you possess in Him remains to be discovered! Your being complete in Christ doesn't mean that it's just fine that you gossip, read your horoscope, and fail every test because you never study. It *does* mean that the power to change—into God's person, not man's ideal—comes from Jesus. The whole idea is captured very well in a simple song.

> In Him is all I need,
> > In Him is all I need.
> His abundance for my emptiness
> > And His life for my lifelessness.
> His love for my coldness
> > And His light for my darkness.
> His truth for my deceit
> > And His joy for my sadness.
> His victory for my defeat
> > And His rest for my restlessness.[2]

And the measuring stick for competence is not: "Have you won any beauty contests lately," "Did you get straight A's on your report card?" or "How many gold medals did you receive?" It's, "What have you received from Jesus lately?"

---

[2]Author unknown

MEMORIZE

"For in him you have been enriched in every way—in all your speaking and in all your knowledge" (1 Cor. 1:5).

VISUALIZE

PERSONALIZE

I, _____ , through God's grace have been enriched in every way—in ability to speak His words and to act in His wisdom.

PRAY THE VERSE, APPLYING IT TO YOUR LIFE

Dear God, thanks that in Jesus you've given me all I need. Help me to discover the treasure of the right words to say and the discernment to do the right thing in _____ (touchy situation).

RECEIVE SOMETHING SPECIAL FROM JESUS TODAY

Meditate on the thought: "For in him you have been enriched in every way." What do you need today? It's already there—but you must receive it.

Confidence Comes on Crutches!

Julie was excited about making the performing marching band. Tryouts were tough and she'd qualified. However, she was scared to death. Having moved from a small town without a marching band, she had to learn fast, or lose her position.

The first practice was a nightmare—it's no fun being the only person out of step. Although she had memorized her music perfectly, she couldn't play a note, because marching took all her concentration.

As they headed for the bandroom, Marilyn caught up with her. "I can help you with your marching," she declared. "You just lack self-confidence. In my self-actualization class, we learned that chanting, 'I'm not afraid—I can do it,' over and over builds self-confidence."

Julie decided to try it, and kept telling herself "I can do it"—until Thursday's practice. But if anything, she did worse the second time. Thoroughly discouraged, she considered quitting.

Most Christians realize that Marilyn's solution to Julie's problem sounds a lot different from the words of Jesus: "Apart from me you can do nothing" (John 15:5). Paul states, "We . . . put no confidence in the flesh" (Phil. 3:2). And in Jer. 17:5 we find, "This is what the Lord says: 'Cursed is the one who trusts in man, who depends on flesh for his strength.' "

The Bible clearly teaches that confidence in what you can do by yourself is misplaced. The world's idea of self-confidence must be scrapped. So often the areas of great natural abilities and confidence become a person's trap. A thrifty person becomes a Scrooge, an easygoing guy ends up being a bum, or a brilliant girl falls into egotism. Any strength or ability used in the wrong way turns into a weakness.

However, the Bible has a lot to say about confidence— that is, confidence in what GOD can do *through* you. Telling a person that *self*-confidence is wrong without adding that it is correct to trust that God can do great things through him or her is like taking away the innertube (and it does have a slow leak) before you teach the person to swim. Paul says, "I am confident in the Lord that I myself will come soon" (Phil. 2:24). He writes to the Thessalonians: "We have confidence in the Lord that you are doing and will continue to do the things we command" (2 Thess. 3:4). Confidence in what *God* will do in you is right, and you need lots of it.

You don't gain confidence by yourself, and God doesn't do it by himself, leaving you out of the picture. "Not that we are competent to claim anything for ourselves, but our competence comes from God" (2 Cor. 3:5).

An illustration might clarify the point. Imagine a pilot announcing to his passengers: "I'm a very confident pilot and I don't need any instruments to fly. That familiar-looking cloud is a sky-mark and I'll get you to Los Angeles in record time!" Ridiculous? But you wouldn't be much happier to hear, "We're landing in this cornfield right now. I no longer believe in the law of aerodynamics and I'll never fly again!" A pilot needs tremendous confidence, but that confidence must be channeled through his flying instruments. In a bad storm, following what the instruments say may even give the pilot the sensation that he is flying upside down. Still he must follow the gages in the cockpit. Only then can he competently guide the airplane.

To be really confident, you do need crutches—and the only support system that will work is God.

MEMORIZE

"To this end I labor, struggling with all his energy, which so powerfully works in me" (Col. 1:29).

VISUALIZE

PERSONALIZE

To accomplish my goal, I work cooperating with all the energy of the Holy Spirit who moves powerfully inside me.

PRAY THE VERSE, APPLYING IT TO YOUR LIFE

Dear God, you know I need to _____ . I know my part is putting forth my effort coordinated with the power of the Holy Spirit who is working in me.

TURN ON THE SWITCH AND EXPERIENCE SOME OF GOD'S POWER

Someone has said, "The hardest part of any job is getting started." In order to sense that God is putting words into your mouth to share Christ with a friend, *you* must start the conversation. To experience "love-your-enemies-love" flowing through you, *you* must buy the plant and give it to Miss Gossip. If you're going to receive God's help to do the chemistry assignment, *you* must open the book and study diligently. Ask God what step you need to take *today*, expecting Him to fill your efforts with supernatural power.

Confidence-Shakers Hit Cement Wall

Mike and Butch came back from the youth retreat ready to evangelize the whole school.

They had decided to start a Bible club that would meet on Tuesday nights at the YMCA, two blocks from school. They printed up flyers and passed out over three hundred invitations. After all their work and planning, only two kids showed up at the meeting, and neither one seemed very interested. Worse than that, Mike and Butch were called to the principal's office and reprimanded for handing out the flyers without receiving school permission. Humiliated and discouraged, they promised to have all flyers approved by the principal's secretary—and they already knew she didn't like Christians. Silently, they headed toward the cafeteria. Like robots, they received their lunch trays and sat down at the nearest table. In a week and a half all their confidence and enthusiasm had evaporated.

Has anything like that ever happened to you? There's a verse that needs to become part of your life—Ps. 27:3: "Though an army besiege me, my heart will not fear; though war break out against me, even then will I be confident." If you have *self*-confidence, everything depends on how self is doing. But if you have your confidence placed in what an all-powerful and unchanging God can do through you, it's possible to see what the psalmist meant. No set of circumstances, however mind-boggling, no problem, however big its teeth, need shake you if your confidence is in God.

Another psalm puts it this way: "Surely he will never be shaken; a righteous man will be remembered forever. He will have no fear of bad news; his heart is steadfast, trusting in the Lord" (Ps. 112:6–7).

And your confidence doesn't have to droop even if your problem takes a long time to be resolved. Maintaining faith when the forecast is for stormy weather isn't easy. Not too many people deserve gold medals for hanging in there when the going gets tough. But the Bible teaches us that we should be so confident in God and what He can do through us that we even welcome difficulties! "Consider it pure joy, my brothers, whenever you face trials of many kinds, because you know that the testing of your faith develops perseverance. Perseverance must finish its work so that you may be mature and complete, not lacking anything" (James 1:2–4).

Introduce the confidence-shakers in your life—the morning news, the unexpected bad report card, that "Dear John" letter, or your mother's cancer operation—to the cement wall; your assurance is that God has everything under control, and He can work through you. Let "though-war-break-out-against-me-even-then-will-I-be-confident" type Bible verses soak into your mind and your spirit. Get excited about the tests designed to teach you patience and perseverance.

Don't get shook. Your confidence is in God and He's a rock, a fortress, a strong tower—and even a bomb shelter!

MEMORIZE

"For everything that was written in the past was written to teach us, so that through endurance and the encouragement of the Scriptures we might have hope" (Rom. 15:4).

VISUALIZE

PERSONALIZE

Everything in the Bible was written for me. My confidence in what God can do through me is built up by sticking with it and the encouragement I find from reading and internalizing God's Word.

PRAY THE VERSE, APPLYING IT TO YOUR LIFE

Thank you for the Bible and the fact that everything in it can help me. Thanks for the hope that's mine if I don't give up but keep receiving encouragement from your Word.

MEDITATE ON SCRIPTURE

Copy this card to carry around with you today. Repeat the verse in your mind every opportunity you get and make it part of you. As you go to sleep, meditate on the verse.

That's the Limit—Or Is It?

Ryan was part of a Christian theater group, and because of his acting ability was always given lead parts. Everyone said he was a natural on the stage and he didn't even get nervous. Invited to put on their production in the Civic Auditorium, all the members of the cast were excited. It was the night they had all waited for.

Arriving just in the nick of time (after having had an argument with his mother), Ryan missed the pre-performance prayer time. He rushed to get into his costume, bounced out on the stage—and forgot his lines. His mind was a total blank! After Jeannie had asked him three times, "And what have you to say today, my dear Richard?" the prompter came to his rescue. Butterflies filled his stomach and he didn't even begin to recover until Act III.

Like Ryan, we all need to learn that confidence isn't something you either have or don't have; it's something you must keep receiving from God. The batteries of whatever *self*-confidence you may have often wear thin. They're either drained or charged by people and circumstances around you. The source of true confidence comes from knowing what an all-powerful God can accomplish *through* you. Because it's placed in a God who can do anything, this confidence doesn't wane.

Receiving from God is the key to true confidence. Because of this, the devil is constantly trying to keep the mail from getting through. A package from heaven is just what you need, and he knows it. If Satan can convince you to limit yourself to your hang-ups and present capabilities, you'll never tap the supernatural power available to you. When fear overtakes you, you've lost it. On the other hand, pride (which is often termed as overconfidence) can defeat you just as easily. Ruts—"This is what I do and this is the way I do it"—can become all too comfortable and so we don't receive from God because we don't ask.

As long as it fits in with His master plan for the universe, God never gets tired of giving to us. God never goes into a "that's-the-limit-I've-given-you-all-I'm-going-to-give-and-now-you're-on-your-own" tirade. It's you who ignores God's offer or tells Him, "Stop! I can't handle any more." God will give you everything you need to carry out His will. If you don't believe it, just read some biographies of the world's greatest missionaries. The only limit is your ability to receive from God.

MEMORIZE

"And God is able to make all grace abound to you, so that in all things at all times, having all you need, you will abound in every good work" (2 Cor. 9:8).

VISUALIZE

PERSONALIZE

God can flood my life with His kindness, mercy, friendship and gifts, which produce love, joy, peace, patience and power in my life, so that I'm ready to face anything because I have all I need from Him.

PRAY THE VERSE, APPLYING IT TO YOUR LIFE

Dear God, thank you that you never run out of grace. Right now I need it for _____ (problem). I claim that I have all I need to be victorious and to overcome evil with good.

DRAW SOME BLUEPRINTS FOR CONTRIBUTING TO THE KINGDOM OF GOD

Prayerfully ask God what He'd like you to do for Him (not limiting yourself because of lack of money, lack of training, or lack of ability). Believe God for "all you need to abound in every good work."

WEEK 10
DAY 2

Self-Examination

1. What problems will you encounter trying to be "Superman Christian" or "Bionic Woman for Jesus?"
   _____ a. You will put yourself under too much pressure, because God created you to work with other Christians and not to be a one-person show.
   _____ b. You will become proud and self-centered.
   _____ c. You'll fail, because you attempted something you were never meant to do.
   _____ d. All of the above.

2. Competence comes from God, but even Jesus "grew in wisdom." So I should expect some frustration in the learning process.   T F
3. Where does the power to live the Christian life that follows a supernatural standard come from?_____
4. What causes the crises of confidence in your life?___
   _____

5. To be confident.
   _____ a. I must believe that I can do it.
   _____ b. I turn off my mind, sit on the sidelines and let God do His miracles. He needs no help from me.
   _____ c. I must try harder next time.

_____ d. I must discard *self*-confidence and replace it with confidence in what God will do *through* me.

6. When something threatens to shake your confidence, what should you do?_____

_____

7. What is the key to true confidence?_____

8. What is my part in gaining competence and confidence?_____

_____

9. How many times this week did you remember that you *are* the light of the world? _____
What happened?_____

10. I should live so that "the name of the Lord Jesus Christ may be _____" in me and I "in Him" (2 Thess. 1:12).

PART 6

In Jesus I Share Everything He Has

We are heirs—heirs of God and co-heirs with Christ.

Romans 8:17

The Title Is Still in Jesus' Name

Bruce was confused. A friend from school had just become involved in a cult which teaches that Jesus was not really God. Bruce knew that Jesus, "being in very nature God, did not consider equality with God something to be grasped, but made himself nothing, taking the very nature of a servant, being made in human likeness" (Phil. 2:6–7). But he didn't know how to fit Rom. 8:29—"For those God foreknew he also predestined to be conformed to the likeness of his Son, that he might be the firstborn among many brothers"—into his theology. He wondered how Christians could be called brothers and sisters of Christ, and he didn't know how to deal with his friend's godlike aspirations.

Maybe you've also struggled to find answers for some of these questions. First of all, we must realize that although Jesus laid aside His total power as God to come to earth, His nature as God did not change. "For in Christ all the fullness of the Deity lives in bodily form" (Col. 2:9). At every point during His earthly life, Jesus deserved the honor due only to God. Wise men worshiped Jesus as a baby. When the blind man who had received his sight found Him, "the man said, 'Lord, I believe,' and he worshiped him" (John 9:38). Jesus accepted the worship He deserved.

But because of His human body and His decision to come to earth, Jesus did not exercise all the rights He had as God. He gave up the prerogative of being in Nazareth, Bethlehem and Jerusalem at the same time. He surrendered the privilege of living independently of earthly elements and experienced hunger and thirst. He could have called legions of angels to rescue Him from the cross; instead, He experienced untold human agony. Jesus had a choice whether or not to obey God. Heb. 2:18 tells us: "Because he himself suffered when he was tempted, he is able to help those who are being tempted." If it had been impossible for Jesus to sin, there would have been no suffering involved. Jesus voluntarily made himself dependent on the Father's life inside Him and declared, "It is the Father, living in me, who is doing His work" (John 14:10).

The most amazing thing is that Jesus came to earth to die and rise again—not only to save us from hell, but to share with us everything He has. "The Spirit himself testifies with our own spirit that we are God's children. Now if we are children, then we are heirs—heirs of God and co-heirs with Christ" (Rom. 8:16–17). It's completely mind-boggling but it's true. Jesus wants to share everything He has with you; for starters: His power, authority, riches, peace and His joy. And you desperately need to see what great changes you'll experience in your daily life when you start acting like a co-heir of Jesus Christ.

Jesus' offer to give us everything He has is like a king deciding that his doorman will share his palace, his money, his power, his honor. The doorman can enjoy his new-found position to the fullest, but he must remember that he is forever indebted to the king. Left on his own, he has nothing. Jesus is willing to give us everything that is His and to treat us as brothers and sisters. But we must never, never, never forget that we are totally God-dependent.

Sure, we get to enjoy using His power and His authority; we can experience His peace and wisdom. But He owns the property, and the title is still in Jesus' name.

The King and I

Scott had just had an argument with his girlfriend, Candi. Their disagreements usually centered around the same theme—being responsible.

They were very different. Scott was the super-conscientious type who carried the weight of the world on his shoulders and felt that each time he neglected to do his duty he had marred his Christian testimony. Candi was just the opposite—carefree, spontaneous and scatter-brained. If she didn't do her homework, she'd shrug and say, "A hundred years from now it won't matter anyway." Being late or inconveniencing others didn't seem to bother her. When everyone showed up at the canceled youth meeting because she forgot to tell them, she passed it off lightly, saying, "Oh, I had so much on my mind I just couldn't remember everything."

This had proved too much for Scott, and he had given her one of his lectures on being responsible. Her comeback had been, "You don't even trust God. You try to be responsible for the entire world."

Scott knew that it was Candi's cheerful lightheartedness that made her attractive to him, and she did have a point. He was probably so caught up in being responsible that he didn't trust God. Yet, at other times he felt that Candi didn't have any more faith than he did. It was just that she took no responsibility for her actions.

What's the right balance? The answer lies in realizing

that you are a co-heir with Jesus and that He wants to let you reign with Him.

That's right! Jesus is sitting in heaven, looking down at every problem as though it were already solved, inviting you to sit beside Him. The Bible says of Christ, "And God placed all things under his feet" (Eph. 1:22). We reign with Jesus: "But because of his great love for us, God, who is rich in mercy, made us alive with Christ . . . And God raised us up with Christ and seated us with him in the heavenly realms in Christ Jesus" (Eph. 2:4–6).

Because Jesus lives in you and you in Him, you have the right to reign with Jesus. Hard chemistry tests, dead batteries, and lost library books don't ruin the kingdom of God. Jesus already knows what to do about these situations, so you need only to ask Him and carry out His instructions. Rom. 5:17 tells us, "Those who receive God's abundant provision of grace and of the gift of righteousness reign in life through one man, Jesus Christ."

You're meant to receive what you need from God and to cooperate with Him so that you reign with Him—over the disappointing change in plans, the missed free-throw that lost the game, or the spot on the new dress that just won't come out.

You're not to be like Candi, who runs her own show, deciding that nothing will cramp her style, or like Scott, enslaved to duty. Jesus and you are to rule over life's circumstances. In order to reign with Jesus, you must get all your instructions from Him and then carry out His ideas. There is no room for irresponsibly letting things slide. But it will be so different from shouldering the whole load and worrying about how things will turn out. You already know that Jesus has it all under control. You only need to follow His directions.

So when everyone shows up at the forest preserve for the picnic you planned *except* the guy who has all the food in the back of his truck, decide: "This is a project for the King and I—together we will reign over the situation because I'll get His mind on how to handle it." If your mother absolutely forbids you to go to church, apply the

"King-and-I" approach to the problem.

Remember, you're reigning with Jesus. Don't abdicate the throne—no matter what.

THE KING'S EARTHLY CROWN

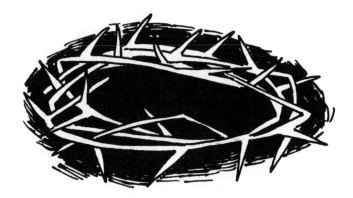

MEMORIZE

"If we endure, we will also reign with him. If we disown him, he will also disown us" (2 Tim. 2:12).

PERSONALIZE

If I keep believing that Jesus has the solution to the problem and keep listening carefully to His instructions, I'll reign with Him over the situation. If I disown Him as the king who reigns over my life by stating that there is no solution, or by making my own rash decisions, He can't let me reign with Him.

PRAY THE VERSE, APPLYING IT TO YOUR LIFE

Dear God, help me hang on, knowing that you have both the solution and instructions for me concerning _____ (problem in your life) so I can keep reigning with you. I'm not going to step down from the throne by _____ (quick action that you know isn't completely right) so you have to disown me as a co-ruler over this situation.

CROWN JESUS KING OF YOUR LIFE

List the ways you've disowned Him this week by manufacturing your own solutions to problems. Determine that when the next situation arises, you'll use the "King-and-I" approach—carrying out the specific instructions Jesus gives you for the occasion.

More Power Than the President of the United States

Lori woke up with a headache. It was the day she had been dreading for three weeks.

She opened her Bible, but she couldn't concentrate. She tried to pray, but she knew she didn't really believe there would be any answer. The English teacher had assigned oral reports that required a great deal of research and had carefully explained that two major tests and *this report* would be the most important grades of the semester. To Lori good grades were worth working for. However, speaking in front of a group was her greatest fear.

Although Lori had carefully done all the research and practiced her presentation countless times, past memories haunted her. Whenever she was ready to give an oral report, she became physically sick. Lori forced herself to go to school. With effort, she entered the classroom and took her seat. Trying to think positively, she attempted to be thankful that English was first hour and that the ordeal would soon be over. But her face was flushed, chills ran up and down her spine, and she was becoming dizzy. Hearing the teacher call her name, she turned white. Only putting her head down on the desk erased the blackness that engulfed her. After a few minutes, the teacher asked two other girls to take Lori to the nurse's office.

Once Lori knew she didn't have to give the speech, she felt better physically. But realizing she had failed again filled her eyes with tears. Right then and there she made up her mind to never try public speaking again.

Do you, like Lori, suffer from an unreasonable fear, from unbelievably mixed-up circumstances, or from inability to cope? Then you need the same truth that could have kept Lori from resigning herself to what she thought was her fate.

The facts that change the seemingly unchangeable are these: First, "Anything that takes us from an attitude of worship, peace, and joy and consciousness of God's presence has a satanic source."[1] Instead of blaming the devil, we accuse our parents of not raising us right. We decide that it's our destiny to suffer constantly. Or we assume guilt that really isn't ours. Not holding the devil responsible for his actions causes untold misery. If the situation isn't a consequence of sin and stubbornness, your first thought should be, "This is an attack of the devil and in the power of Jesus I can resist it." (If the situation *is* a case of sin and stubbornness, you need to repent.)

Second, because you are a co-heir of Christ, He has voluntarily shared His power with you. And His power over Satan is complete. The devil has already been defeated. It might seem too good to be true, but Jesus really said it and it's right there in your Bible: "I tell you the truth, anyone who has faith in me will do what I have been doing. He will do even greater things than these because I am going to the Father" (John 14:12). This verse isn't just for the apostles. It's for *anyone* who has faith. It's for *you*.

And what did Jesus do? Acts 10:38 tells us: "How God anointed Jesus of Nazareth with the Holy Spirit and power, and how he went around doing good and healing all who were under the power of the devil, because God was with him."

A good place to start is your own life. If Jesus came into your room right now, what would you ask Him to do

---

[1]Sarah Foulkes Moore, *Our Throne Rights* (Los Angeles, Calif.: Free Tract Society Inc.), p. 12.

for you? In what way is the devil messing up your life? In Jesus' name, take authority over Satan. Use the power Jesus has given you and share the joy of the seventy-two who returned from their evangelism tour, exclaiming, "Lord, even the demons submit to us in your name" (Luke 10:17).

You might not have been informed of your inheritance, but Jesus has left you more power than any president of the United States—that is, unless he, too, is a Christian.

WE HAVE THE VICTORY

MEMORIZE

"May the God of hope fill you with all joy and peace as you trust in him, so that you may overflow with hope by the power of the Holy Spirit" (Rom. 15:13).

PERSONALIZE

God wants me, _____, to be filled with joy, and peace and hope—not to feel hemmed in by problems and trials. Because the same Holy Spirit who gave power to Jesus lives in me, no situation is hopeless.

PRAY THE VERSE, APPLYING IT TO YOUR LIFE

Dear God, fill me with hope and joy and peace. I trust you to _____ (solve your biggest problem). Thank you for the power of the Holy Spirit, which gives me power over the devil and his attempts to wreck things for me.

MEDITATE ON SCRIPTURE

Copy this card and take it along with you today. Put this verse into your mind and your spirit. Let it make changes in your life. Go to sleep meditating on the verse.

All This and Heaven Too!

Turn on your imagination and take a trip back in time.

The year is 1932. Clyde lived on a Kansas farm. Drought and depression made the struggle for survival very fierce indeed. Even during "good times," Clyde's family possessed very little. Now they had even less. Conditioned since birth to accept poverty as a way of life, Clyde expected very little.

Then one day word came that Clyde's great-uncle, who had gone to South Africa to mine diamonds and gold, had named him as heir. A check came for $500 million with the explanation that this was just guarantee money which he could use until all his great-uncle's mines were sold and he came into his full inheritance!

Can you imagine a boy like Clyde suddenly receiving all that money? Will it be easy for him to break out of his thought patterns and habits to live a new life? What will he do with such riches?

You may never have fully realized it, but you're a Clyde with a similar inheritance. Eph. 1:13–14 tells us, "Having believed, you were marked in him with a seal, the promised Holy Spirit, who is a deposit guaranteeing our inheritance until the redemption of those who are God's possession—to the praise of his glory." As a born-again Christian, you are a co-heir with Jesus. You'll get to share all the excitement of heaven with Him.

Jesus told His disciples: "In my Father's house are many rooms" (John 14:2)—and as a co-heir yours will be just as beautiful as the one reserved for Jesus! And you'll get just as much love, acceptance and attention from God the Father as Jesus receives. Heaven will be so wonderful you can't even imagine it! "No eye has seen, no ear has heard, no mind has conceived what God has prepared for those who love him" (1 Cor. 2:9). It'll do your heart good to spend some time once in a while thinking about heaven.

But so many people forget all about the Holy Spirit, "who is a deposit guaranteeing our inheritance." If we would only break out of our "I'm-a-pitiful-creature-waiting-for-pie-in-the-sky-by-and-by" mentality and receive what the Holy Spirit wants to give us here and now, heaven can begin on earth. "But the fruit of the Spirit is love, joy, peace, patience, kindness, goodness, faithfulness, gentleness and self-control" (Gal. 5:22–23). If you truly permit the Holy Spirit to place these virtues in your life, you'll spread a little heaven wherever you go.

Jesus told His disciples, "But you will receive power when the Holy Spirit comes on you" (Acts 1:8). And that great energy from the Holy Spirit has been available to believers ever since. The same power that raised Jesus from the dead lives in you (Eph. 1:17–20). It's the power you've always wanted to live a victorious Christian life, to win your world for Jesus and to love your little brother. Besides the complete set of Christlike qualities and dynamite power, the Holy Spirit gives specific spiritual gifts to Christians—your special present from God. "There are different kinds of gifts, but the same Spirit . . . now to each one the manifestation of the Spirit is given for the common good" (1 Cor. 12:4, 7). Do a Bible study on spiritual gifts and open yourself to let the gifts of the Spirit operate through you. (Do remember that there is no place for pride or for spiritual talent shows. The purpose of a spiritual gift is to strengthen your Christian life and that of others. There is only one celebrity—Jesus Christ. And the Holy Spirit *always* focuses on Him.)

Start taking advantage of all you can receive through "the deposit guaranteeing your inheritance," the precious Holy Spirit. Live like a co-heir of Christ, receiving more and more from the Holy Spirit each day. His blessings are yours to enjoy—all this and heaven too!

BREAK THIS MENTALITY

MEMORIZE

"And if the Spirit of him who raised Jesus from the dead is living in you, he who raised Christ from the dead will also give life to your mortal bodies through his Spirit, who lives in you" (Rom. 8:11).

PERSONALIZE

Because I've invited Jesus into my life, the Holy Spirit who raised Jesus from the dead lives in me. The life of the Holy Spirit with Christlike qualities, power, strength and special God-given abilities to help other Christians operates in my physical body. It's my body, but His life.

PRAY THE VERSE, APPLYING IT TO YOUR LIFE

Dear God, thank you that the Holy Spirit who raised Jesus from the dead lives in me. Right now my body is having problems and needs the life of the Holy Spirit for _____ . I receive your life in my body.

TELL YOUR BODY THAT IT'S NO LONGER BOSS

Explain to your body that its desires must be subject to Jesus and that its laziness and indulgence will be eradicated by the life of Jesus within. Remember that Jesus in you has supernatural power.

". . . Or Are You Going to Spend the Rest of Your Life Watching Television?"

Jessica was in charge of the homecoming assembly. For weeks she worked so everything would come off just right. She and her friends spent hours practicing a skit. She hunted up talent from the student body that others didn't even know about. A lot of students participated, and the performance went like clockwork. When it was all over, only a couple of friends complimented her on the fine job she had done. But basically she was exhausted, and wondered what she had really accomplished. By Monday morning no one even remembered that there had been a homecoming assembly.

Do you, like Jessica, sometimes wonder if you're doing anything worthwhile with your time? Do school assignments, unironed clothes and lists of things to do form a cycle of meaninglessness that keeps on being repeated week after week?

If so, you need to pay attention to these words of Jesus: "I no longer call you servants because a servant does not know his master's business. Instead, I have called you friends, for everything that I learned from my Father I have made known to you" (John 15:15). As a Christian and co-heir of Christ you get to share His work—not as a servant who just follows orders with no idea what's going on but as a partner whose contribution to the kingdom of God is important. If you can only catch a glimpse of what it means to be involved in the Great Commission, "Go into all the world and preach the good news to all creation" (Mark 16:15), your life will never be boring again.

Your classmate could stop taking drugs and spend all eternity in heaven just because you cared enough to share Jesus with him. The girl who is ready to commit suicide can give her heart to Jesus and find peace and courage to face life because you gave an extra offering to keep that Christian broadcast on the air. The neighbor kid from a broken home can grow up experiencing Christ's love and purpose for living because you took time to evangelize him and invite him to your house once a week for Bible stories and Christian teaching. The letter you write to the school secretary who just lost her husband can show her that there is hope in Christ and a new way to live. You really can cooperate with Jesus to change your world for the better.

Not only has Jesus chosen to give you His Holy Spirit so you can work with Him as a partner in transforming lives, but you can help populate heaven! You have the privilege of spending your time and energy accomplishing great things for time and eternity.

You're young. You can choose how you want to live your life. You can take seriously the call of Jesus to share His work. Are you going to invest your time in spreading the life-changing message that sets alcoholics free, gives hope to the lonely and changes eternal destinies? Or are you going to spend the rest of your life watching television? It's your choice.

PRIORITIZE YOUR LIFE

MEMORIZE

"The man who plants and the man who waters have one purpose, and each will be rewarded according to his own labor. For we are God's fellow workers" (1 Cor. 3:8–9).

PERSONALIZE

Only God can put eternal life in people. But I can plant seeds and water them. God will reward me for my work because I'm cooperating with Him in bringing people to Jesus.

PRAY THE VERSE, APPLYING IT TO YOUR LIFE

Dear God, thank you for making me your co-worker and giving me the privilege of doing work that will count for eternity. Show me how to plant a seed for _____ (name of friend) to come to Jesus and to water the seed already planted in _____ .

JOIN GOD'S "WE'RE-OUT-TO-CHANGE-THE-WORLD" TEAM

Remember that all the power comes from God, but He loves us so much that He chose to work through us to bring good news and new life to classmates, neighbors, and relatives. Decide right now to revise your schedule and rearrange your priorities to become part of an exciting adventure—contributing time, money, and effort to bring the gospel to all the world.

WEEK 11
DAY 3

Writing Checks From the World's Biggest Bank Account

Rick usually considered social studies his favorite subject. But this year he found it downright depressing.

The dangers of nuclear war, AIDS, air pollution and communism had been duly discussed. Now they were studying overpopulation and impending worldwide economic disaster.

Rick even dreamed that he lived in an extremely crowded city where no food was available except cans of sauerkraut and packages of Oreo cookies! The dream was so real that he raided the refrigerator the minute he woke up and ate nine pancakes for breakfast. Then he went to first-hour class and heard the teacher proclaim that it would soon be impossible to feed the world's population and that global hunger would create revolutions which would put an end to civilization as we know it.

If you've ever wondered about your future in a world of shortages, unpaid national debts and inflation, you need to remember that as a co-heir with Jesus there's a verse you can claim literally: "And my God will meet all your needs according to his glorious riches in Christ Jesus" (Phil. 4:19). There are some things to remember when considering this verse.

Although it is certainly not incorrect to interpret it in terms of emotional and spiritual needs, the context speaks of material needs. Because it says God will meet *all* your needs, it starts right now, not after you get to heaven. And the verse states that your needs are met from a fund called "glorious riches in Christ Jesus"—a supply that will never run short. Jesus offers to share His bank account with you.

Because there are some extreme teachings on this subject, many ignore it altogether. While there is no verse in the Bible that affirms that Cadillacs, Caribbean cruises and Christians go together, there are promises that God will take care of His children regardless of the world's economic situation. However, God's promises come true only for those who believe them. You have salvation because you put your faith in the fact that "everyone who calls on the name of the Lord will be saved" (Rom. 10:13). And you acted on it.

God's other promises work the same way. As you claim God's provisions for your economic well-being, it is important to remember that the wise heavenly Father, not unlike many earthly fathers with huge fortunes, knows when and how to give you from His bounty. If you have not learned His principles of living, too much prosperity could be very dangerous for you. God will give to you on His terms, not yours.

There is no place in the Christian's life for fear of the economic future. God gives you His word: "The days of the blameless are known to the Lord, and their inheritance will endure forever. In times of disaster they will not wither, in days of famine they will enjoy plenty" (Ps. 37:18–19). That promise is for you.

But there's a condition: It's a promise for the *blameless*—those who have made it their business to study the Bible, to know what God requires and to live by His rules.

Because you're a co-heir with Jesus, you get to draw from the world's biggest bank account! First of all, thank God for this fact and decide not to worry about your future security. Then determine to get to know God and His Word so well that the regulations of the Bank of Heaven become known to you.

MEMORIZE

"But his delight is in the law of the Lord, and on his law he meditates day and night. He is like a tree planted by streams of living water, which yields its fruit in season and whose leaf does not wither. Whatever he does prospers" (Ps. 1:2–3).

VISUALIZE

PERSONALIZE

I want to find my joy in God's Word and meditate on it day and night. Then I'll be like a tree planted by the river of God's abundance, and I won't be dependent on the world around me. Then I will be prosperous.

PRAY THE VERSE, APPLYING IT TO YOUR LIFE

Dear God, thank you for your Word. I plan to make it my delight by meditating on it constantly. This will show me how to receive prosperity from the river of God's abundance regardless of the world's economic situation and scary news of _____ .

MEDITATE ON SCRIPTURE

Copy this card and carry it with you. Use each free moment to meditate on this verse and work it into your daily life. Think about it as you go to sleep.

Make Your Whole Life a Treasure Hunt!

Roger realized that he had made a terrible mistake. After hearing a rousing sermon on faith, he decided to get the Christian kids at his school together to rent the auditorium and to show a Christian film. They passed out flyers with the headline: FREE SATURDAY NIGHT MOVIE.

Not knowing the screen would feature a Christian message, students jammed the auditorium. However, as soon as the movie theme song gave them a clue, kids began to leave in droves. Some shouted their disapproval and made fun of the movie. When it was over, only the Christians and two junior high girls were left. The offering that was to pay the rental fee came to $2.83. To top it off, school officials were angry with Roger because he hadn't told them he planned to use the auditorium for a religious event. He had broken a school board regulation.

As Roger contemplated how he had gotten into the whole mess in the first place, he realized that he had never really prayed for guidance. He had just assumed that anything that might spread the gospel was automatically a good idea. He was "into" faith and spiritual power. Roger made the mistake that so many of us make. We forget that Jesus wants to share His wisdom with us. We don't realize how desperately we need His ways of doing things. We don't *dis*trust our human inclinations enough.

Jesus' disciples loved Him enough to give up everything to follow Him wherever He went. They had good intentions and they were sincere. But let's look at some of their ideas for building God's kingdom. James and John were excited about sharing Jesus' power and wanted to call down fire from heaven to destroy the Samaritans who had not welcomed Jesus to their village. Peter proposed leaving people in need in order to erect three shelters on a mountaintop for two people who already lived in heaven and One who was just about ready to take up permanent residence there! The disciples tried to chase all the children away so Jesus could preach to adults only.

You might think your plans and schemes are far superior to those of the apostles. But if you don't check them out with Jesus, they may do more harm than good. When you think of your position as co-heir with Christ, it's easy to concentrate on power, prosperity and authority. But the *first* thing you need from Jesus is wisdom. "Wisdom is supreme; therefore get wisdom. Though it cost all you have, get understanding" (Prov. 4:7). Jesus is our wisdom. "It is because of him that you are in Christ Jesus, who has become for us wisdom from God" (1 Cor. 1:30). You can get Jesus' wisdom only by admitting that you don't have any (a pretty tough pill to swallow, especially if you are a senior), and asking Jesus for His. Without the wisdom of Jesus your Christian life will never be a success. Col. 2:2–3 puts it this way: ". . . Christ, in whom are hidden all the treasures of wisdom and knowledge."

Decide to make your whole life a treasure hunt, searching out the deep wisdom of Jesus. He gladly shares His knowledge with those who look for it. "Wisdom is supreme; therefore get wisdom."

MEMORIZE

"If any of you lacks wisdom, he should ask God, who gives generously to all without finding fault, and it will be given him" (James 1:5).

VISUALIZE

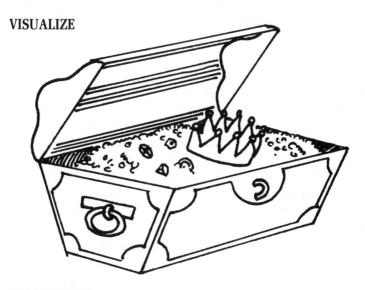

PERSONALIZE

I need wisdom for _____ , _____ , and _____ . I will ask God, knowing He won't put me down for my ignorance. God will give me the wisdom I need.

PRAY THE VERSE, APPLYING IT TO YOUR LIFE

Dear God, thank you that you want to give me wisdom. _____ is a big problem and I need wisdom. I'm planning to _____ , but I need your guidance. Is it the right thing to do? Thank you that you will give me the wisdom I need.

WISE UP BY DUMPING YOUR KNOW-IT-ALL ATTITUDE

How many times this month have you seriously refused to consider advice? (Be honest.) How may times have you really asked God for advice before making your purchases, deciding how to spend your Saturdays, and choosing your friends? Do you really sense a need for God's wisdom? Pray about this question and ask God to change your know-it-all attitude.

Peace on Earth, Anyone?

Cristina finally arrived home at 9:30 P.M. She had been rushing all day.

Having risen at 5:30 that morning to write an English essay before breakfast, she was tired when she left for school. The day was filled with noisy hallways, warning bells, end-of-the hour buzzers, lunchroom chaos, classroom disorder and pressure—always more pressure. After school, her supervisor insisted that she work extra hours in the department store where December shoppers never gave her one minute's rest.

She arrived home frazzled and frustrated, wishing she could spend the rest of her life skiing silently down a mountainside. On the table was a blue envelope with her name on it. Inside was a beautiful blue and gold Christmas card that said, "Peace on Earth. Good will to men. Jesus is our peace." Cristina sighed. Peace was certainly what she needed. She was sure that Jesus had plenty of it. But how could she get some?

Peace is not dependent on circumstances. If it were, most of us would have to wait until heaven before we'd get any. It is always wrong to say to yourself, "It's only natural that I should feel tense and depressed, considering everything that's going on right now." Because you are a new creature, you have the supernatural life of Jesus within you. As a co-heir with Him, you get to share all that He has, and one of these things is His peace. You receive peace as a gift. Jesus declared, "Peace I leave with you; my peace I give you. I do not give to you as the world gives. Do not let your hearts be troubled and do not be afraid" (John 14:27).

Receiving the gift of peace involves the conscious decision to ignore the chaotic circumstances and accept the peace Jesus offers. Paul tells people at Colosse, "Let the peace of Christ rule in your hearts" (Col. 3:15).

It comes down to a determination to live by faith in God's promises, regardless of how much our emotions protest. Telling your emotions that they're out to lunch and setting your will to let the peace of Christ rule in your heart will not be easy—especially at first. Your emotions will always try to become dictator of your personality. The sad thing is that most of us are accustomed to letting this happen. Breaking the bad habit of letting your emotions dominate your life is a must, or you'll never enjoy God's peace.

The Bible is the truth, and it says, "Do not fear." "Do not let your hearts be troubled." Your emotions will scream, "I can't help being scared, nervous and upset!" Your will must intervene: "I'll live by the Bible, not by my emotions. I'll let the peace of Jesus rule my heart."

Peace is the gift Jesus wants to give you, but He doesn't just pass it out like candy. ("Peace on earth, anyone?") It's a big package containing enough peace to fill your entire being. It can be received only as you drop everything else you're carrying—the right to order your own circumstances, the insistence that you understand everything that's happening and a control of your surrender to Jesus. And whenever you decide to pick up a worry, a resentment, or a fear, you have to set down the package marked *Peace*.

Part of your inheritance in Jesus is His peace. But if you're not willing to drop everything and come with empty hands to receive, it will never be yours.

MEMORIZE

"Do not be anxious about anything, but in everything by prayer and petition, with thanksgiving, present your requests to God. And the peace of God, which transcends all understanding, will guard your hearts and your minds in Christ Jesus" (Phil. 4:6–7).

VISUALIZE

PERSONALIZE

I will not worry. God tells me not to. I will pray about everything, thanking God for the answer even before I receive it. I will receive God's peace even though there are things I don't understand. Peace will guard my heart and mind from the thoughts provoked by frustration.

PRAY THE VERSE, APPLYING IT TO YOUR LIFE

Dear God, I will not worry about _____ (big problem), but I ask you to take care of it and thank you for your answer. I receive your peace, which will guard my thoughts and keep me from trying to figure out the solution on my own.

PRAY YOUR WORRIES AWAY

Talk to the Lord about each concern you have, thanking God in advance that since He created the whole universe, He can certainly handle your problem. Because God can be trusted to take charge of the things you worry about, take a vacation at the resort called PEACE.

Self-Examination

1. How can you reconcile the fact that Jesus is God with the fact that while He was on earth, He experienced limitations? _____

2. In what sense are we called brothers and sisters of Christ?_____

3. Describe the "King-and-I" approach to life. _____

4. If the situation that robs your peace wasn't caused by your sin, what should be your first thought? _____

5. We are co-heirs with Christ. What's the guarantee of that inheritance which is ours to enjoy right now?
   _____

6. What's the most worthwhile thing you can do with your life? _____

7. God promises that the blameless will never go hungry.   T   F

8. What is the *first* thing you as a co-heir with Christ should ask Jesus to share with you?_____

9. How do you receive God's peace? _____
   _____
   _____

10. God will give you everything you need
    _____ a. To be the smartest, the richest, and the best looking.
    _____ b. If you're His pet.
    _____ c. If you never sin.
    _____ d. In order to do His will.

---

1. Jesus voluntarily gave up His power as God to take on a human body and depend on the life of His Father within Him. But He never sinned and was at all times worthy of the honor due only to God (John 5:18-19; Phil. 2:5-11; 2 Cor. 5:21; John 9:37-38). 2. It's because He voluntarily chose to share everything He has with us. But the title is still in Jesus' name and we must depend on Him for all we have. 3. I really believe that God has raised me with Christ and seated me with Him in the heavenly realms in Christ Jesus, so I give each problem to Jesus and reign with Him over all the circumstances of my life. 4. This is from the devil and I have authority over Him in Jesus' name. 5. The Holy Spirit, through whom God wants to give me power, joy, and victory. 6. Invest it in bringing others to Jesus—being His co-worker. 7. T 8. Wisdom (Prov. 4:7). 9. By dropping everything else you have and taking it by faith. 10. d.

PART 7

In Jesus I Am Loved

*As the Father has loved me, so have I
loved you.*

John 15:9

I Just Don't Have Time to Fall in Love

Gina really appreciated Diana's friendship. Extremely popular at school and at church, Diana didn't have to take time for Gina, but she did. When Gina asked her how she could make more friends, Diana sat down with her to have a serious talk.

"Gina," she began, "you have to learn to think of others rather than yourself. What do they want to do? What would make them happy? You have to be willing to give, even if you don't get anything in return. You can't always be thinking about how others treat you. You're so quick to show your hurt feelings every time they don't react the way you think they should."

Gina began to cry. "But I don't have any love to give away. I was born when my mother was fifteen. She didn't really want me, so my grandparents raised me. I've heard them say over and over that they should be enjoying their retirement instead of raising another teenager. My psychiatrist says I can't reach out to others because I haven't received real love and acceptance from my family."

If anything Gina said fits you, there's some good news. "This is love: not that we loved God, but that he loved us and sent his Son as an atoning sacrifice for our sins" (1 John 4:10). No one could ever love you the way Jesus does. His love letter to you was written with His blood. He offers to be with you every second of your life—loving you, guiding and supporting you. He asks you to come away with Him to heaven to live forever and forever. His love never grows cold, no matter what you do. He never forgets about you in order to pay attention to someone else. There's more than enough of His love to satisfy every person on earth. He keeps loving you when everyone else gives up on you. "God is love and if you have His life, you are going to have His love."[1]

God's love is the answer for all the Ginas of this world. Even those of us who have parents who really love us realize that the best of human love is imperfect. We, too, need the deep love of Jesus to penetrate the places where human love cannot reach.

Are you like the girl who said, "I just don't have time to fall in love"? Are you too taken up with your friends and your activities to sit at the feet of Jesus and receive His love? Will His love letter to you go unanswered? Are you refusing His gifts and ignoring His overtures of affection? Jesus is the answer to the love shortage. If you cling to your independence, however, and to your busy schedule, you'll still be singing "nobody-loves-me" songs.

Take time to fall in love with Jesus—and then let that love overflow to those around you.

[1]Dr. Paul G. Trulin, *Resurrection Life* (Sacramento, Calif.: Harvesters Missionary Society, 1984), p. 15.

A New Frontier for You to Explore

Lily thought back over her day. At least she was still alive!

Her parents had had a terrible argument at the breakfast table. Then she had forgotten her math book and her homework assignments. When Pam showed up at her locker wearing the brightest yellow blouse she'd ever seen, without thinking Lily blurted: "If you wore that blouse every day, the sun would have to go out of business!"

Pam had burst into tears. "I was worried that the color was too intense. I'll just go home and change." Once again Lily's big mouth had gotten her into trouble.

Her sixth-hour teacher was in a bad mood and gave a long assignment that no one knew how to do. Her girls' basketball team lost their game 66 to 21. And when she came home, she discovered that her cat was sick. Insecurity, feelings of failure, inadequacy and fear overcame her.

Was your day that bad? Even if it wasn't, you need a strategy for handling the emotions Lily faced. Read 2 Thess. 3:5, which points us in the right direction: "May the Lord direct your hearts into God's love." Do you receive His love for your insecurity, retreat into His love when you've failed, and meditate on His love when your weaknesses or fears threaten to do you in? Or do you tend to view God as just any other person who gets exasperated by your lack of confidence, stands ready to lecture you for each little mistake, and is running out of patience because you don't learn faster? Just because nobody else particularly wants to be around you during your bad moments, do you also keep your distance from God? That's not how a Christian is supposed to live.

Paul's prayer, recorded in Eph. 3:17–19, shows us a better way: "And I pray that you, being rooted and established in love, may have power, together with all the saints, to grasp how wide and long and high and deep is the love of Christ, and to know this love that surpasses knowledge—that you may be filled to the measure of all the fullness of God."

Let God's love light up your life. Receive His word: "For his compassions never fail. They are new every morning: great is your faithfulness" (Lam. 3:22–23). Don't start the day without a "love injection" from God. Instead of beating yourself over the head for your mistakes, internalize the truth of Ps. 103:8: "The Lord is compassionate and gracious, slow to anger, abounding in love." In the middle of fears and doubts, hang on to this: "May your love and your truth always protect me" (Ps. 40:11). God's love has depths that you have never probed. It has heights that you have never scaled. It's so wide you have never seen its boundaries. Decide to spend the rest of your life getting to know more and more about the love of God. The exciting thing is that God's love is limitless. There are always new facets to explore and deeper experiences of His caring and concern. God's love has dimensions that satisfy the craving for acceptance and intimacy that human love can't touch.

It's not true that you're locked into life. God's love is a new frontier filled with treasures like compassion, mercy, acceptance and understanding. By making the resources of His love yours, you'll find security, a feeling of worth and enough leftover love to give freely to others. You can keep exploring until you die, but you'll never discover all the wealth available to you.

Determine to dedicate your life to uncovering the riches contained in the love of God.

YOU'RE NOT LOCKED INTO LIFE

MEMORIZE

"By day the Lord directs his love, at night his song is with me—a prayer to the God of my life" (Ps. 42:8).

PERSONALIZE

I will receive God's love. I need it because _____ and _____ (difficult situations or feelings of being misunderstood). I will sing the song you give me as a special prayer to you.

PRAY THE VERSE, APPLYING IT TO YOUR LIFE

Dear God, I receive all the love you send to me every day. Part of that love is the song you give to me, even in the blackness, which becomes a prayer, returning the love you first expressed to me.

DAILY DISCOVER THE LOVE THE LORD
DIRECTS TOWARD YOU

List all the little ways God said "I love you" this week. Then write down all the times you missed His love because you let boredom, anger, depression, or frustration dominate your thinking. Decide to look for God's love at every turn—it's always there.

Throw Away Your Heart-Shaped Umbrella

Vanessa wished that life were like a television set and that she could just switch channels.

Her father was going into the hospital on Tuesday for a cancer operation. Although she knew that her all-powerful God was in control of the situation, the fear of losing her dad kept coming back. Her boyfriend, Ted, was moving to New York. As she would sit in American history class, she'd stare at the big U.S. map on the wall. California and New York were so far apart that he might as well be moving to China. Everyone predicted that no teenage romance could survive such a test.

Besides all this, her name had appeared on the list of students that would be bussed to the neighboring high school in order to equalize student population in the two buildings. Her two best friends, Rachel and Ginger, would be staying at their present school, and Vanessa was lonesome already.

Wasn't there someone she could depend on? Wasn't there anything that spelled security?

There is a love that won't ever let you down. Paul tells the Romans, "For I am convinced that neither death nor life, neither angels nor demons, neither the present nor the future, nor any powers, neither height nor depth, nor anything else in all creation, will be able to separate us from the love of God that is in Christ Jesus our Lord" (Rom.

8:38–39). The love of God is forever.

When you sin, God still loves you. If you make a fool of yourself, you can count on the love of God. Your bad breath, nervous cough, or stammering tongue will not alienate you from God's love. Giving wrong answers, fumbling the ball, or coming late won't affect God's great love for you one bit. And you can't even run away from God's love or turn it off if you try. The psalmist tells God what it's like to be constantly pursued by his love: "Where can I go from your Spirit? Where can I flee from your presence? If I go to the heavens, you are there, if I make my bed in the depths, you are there. If I rise on the wings of the dawn, if I settle on the far side of the sea, even there your hand will guide me, your right hand will hold me fast" (Ps. 139:7–10). God *is* love, and wherever you go or whatever you do, you'll keep bumping into His love.

You can merely accept this fact, or you can enjoy it. It's a little bit like the weather—you can simply live through it, or you can stop to appreciate it. The snow glittering in the sunshine, the refreshing soft spring breeze, the spectacular show put on by a thunder storm, and the crispness of a November day can be yours to treasure. In the same way, you can revel in God's love. You can run into His arms after an especially hard day, draw strength from His presence to face a crisis, bask in the wonder of His love on a lazy afternoon, and return to the verses that declare His love for you to ease the pain inflicted by the harsh words you just heard.

Do you treat God's love with indifference, or do you enjoy every minute of it? "God has poured out his love into our hearts by the Holy Spirit" (Rom. 5:5). Do you own a heart-shaped umbrella that deflects all those love showers, continuing to harden your heart? Or have you thrown away that umbrella so you can soak it all in?

SOAK IN HIS LOVE

MEMORIZE

"We meditate on your unfailing love. Like your name, O God, your praise reaches to the ends of the earth; your right hand is filled with righteousness" (Ps. 48:9–10).

PERSONALIZE

I will constantly think about your unfailing love. I will join people all over the world in giving you honor. I will remember that your ways are right.

PRAY THE VERSE, APPLYING IT TO YOUR LIFE

Dear God, help me always to meditate on your never-ending love whenever I face a love shortage. I praise you for _____ , and _____ . _____ seems unfair, so I'm looking to you because your right hand is filled with righteousness. And you love me.

MEDITATE ON SCRIPTURE

Copy this card so you can think about this verse throughout the day. Let it change you. Go to sleep thinking about the verse.

Fifteen Tons of Pure Smush

Tina was excited because her married sister, whom she hadn't seen for three years, was coming for a visit. She was bringing her two-year-old boy with her.

When Tina saw her little nephew for the first time, she squealed with delight. Robbie was absolutely the cutest little boy she'd ever seen. When her sister gave him a swat for trying to take his grandmother's china out of the cupboard, Tina thought she was cruel. It almost broke her heart to see him cry. Tina thought she loved that little nephew too much to ever spank him.

One afternoon, her sister left to have lunch with her girlfriends, and Tina volunteered to babysit Robbie. She took him out into the yard to play. The first thing he did was run out into the street. Tina ran after him, picked him up, gave him a hug and sweetly said, "Robbie, you mustn't play in the street. It's dangerous." There were two or three repeat performances.

Then the telephone rang. Without thinking, Tina ran in to answer it. Returning a minute later, she saw Robbie lying in the street. He had been hit by a car!

Afterward, in the hospital room, she told her mother the whole story. "But, Tina," her mother scolded, "don't you love Robbie enough to discipline him and keep him from danger?"

"I guess I never thought of it that way," replied Tina. "I thought the only way I could demonstrate love was by being a softie."

What's your idea of love? Does it include restraint, discipline and commands? What does "God is love" really mean? Do you understand that because He loves you, He'll give you rules to live by? Do you realize that He shows His love in a predictable universe that includes consequences for breaking his regulations and blessings for keeping them? Do you see that often things are withheld from you so God can teach you patience? Or do you expect Him to shower you with fifteen tons of pure *smush*?

God loves you so much that He wants to keep you out of trouble—*and* out of hell. What He told the church in Laodicea, He says to you: "Those whom I love I rebuke and discipline" (Rev. 3:19). Heb. 12:10–11 gives an explanation: "God disciplines us for our good, that we may share in his holiness. No discipline seems pleasant at the time, but painful. Later on, however, it produces a harvest of righteousness and peace for those who have been trained by it."

God is not in the business of raising spoiled brats. In fact, the over-pampered child faces life with a handicap as real as an amputated arm or a serious allergy. The undisciplined person suffers all his life from things like disorganization, inability to take orders and ineffectiveness in disciplining others. Because He loves His children so much, God gives them proper discipline so they will be equipped to face life.

Aren't you glad that God loves you enough to see that you receive the discipline you need? Isn't it neat that God won't let your rough edges go unattended? The new you deep inside has to break those bad habits, wrong thought patterns and old reactions. God's wise and loving discipline is designed as surgery to remove the cancerous thought, so your mind can be filled with right ideas. God spanks you so you can't unthinkingly fall back into the same old habit. God's scolding isn't the result of His having had a bad day! In love He gives warnings that will save you from heartbreak and failure.

Be thankful that God's love isn't pure *smush*. Learn to appreciate the purpose of His discipline.

MEMORIZE

"My son, do not make light of the Lord's discipline, and do not lose heart when he rebukes you, because the Lord disciplines those he loves, and he punishes everyone he accepts as a son" (Heb. 12:5–6).

VISUALIZE

PERSONALIZE

I will not push aside God's discipline. I won't get discouraged when God disciplines me because He loves me and punishes me only so I can be a son (daughter) who acts like my Father.

PRAY THE VERSE, APPLYING IT TO YOUR LIFE

Dear God, help me to recognize your discipline and accept it. Keep me from being discouraged when you reprimand me, remembering that you punish all your children because you love them.

DECIDE TO LEARN FROM GOD'S DISCIPLINE

How has God disciplined you lately? Why do you think He had to reprimand you? Have you determined to learn from this situation to avoid a repeat in the future?

Putting "I Love You" Into Practice

Focused on her June wedding for the Saturday after graduation, Joy was so much in love that she didn't even notice other people existed—much less consider their advice. She married Chuck against her parents' wishes and contrary to the counsel of all her trusted Christian friends.

She would never forget the first time she saw him. He had come from the big city in his sports car to visit his cousin next door. Noticing how handsome he was, she tried to attract his attention. He started talking to her over the backyard fence, and then asked her out for dinner. Never had she been treated like such a queen.

Soon weekend dates with Chuck became the highlight of her life. He was so romantic and charming. She had felt she could never live without him.

Six months after the wedding, she found herself in a small apartment in the city, with a husband who was out of work. Whenever she'd mention that he'd better look for a job, he'd laugh, take her in his arms and tell her how much he loved her.

Then he left for a whole week without telling her where he was going. When he returned she demanded an explanation, but he cooed, "It doesn't matter now that we're together again."

Finally she yelled, "Chuck, there's nothing in the place to eat except a bottle of ketchup and a box of crackers. I don't want to starve."

Chuck's reply was, "We're in love, and that's all that matters."

Joy at last turned to her Bible, and the words she read were first spoken by Jesus to His disciples: "If you love me, you will obey what I command" (John 14:15). Now, finally, she saw what they meant.

She had treated Jesus the same way Chuck was treating her. She had told Him she loved Him, and then disobeyed His commandments: "Do not be yoked together with un-believers" (2 Cor. 6:14); "Do not be wise in your own eyes" (Prov. 3:7); and "Love the Lord your God with all your heart and with all your soul and with all your mind and with all your strength" (Mark 12:30).

Joy knew she'd have to face some dreadful conse-quences because of her rebellion, but she also knew that she could come back to Jesus and receive forgiveness. From now on, she would show Jesus she loved Him *by her actions*, not just by what she said.

Like Joy, have you sung praises to Jesus, told Him you loved Him—and then turned to go your own way? Have you given your testimony at church, and acted like a pa-gan at the beach? Have you professed one thing to your Christian friends, and exactly the opposite to the kids at lunch?

If you have been a hypocrite, you need to ask for God's forgiveness. But you also have to learn about another di-mension of God's love. "It's difficult to describe love: you can only recognize it by its actions."[1]

Because this is true, God didn't print "I love you" on every other page of the Bible. Instead, He demonstrated His love in the clearest possible way: He sent Jesus to die for you.

Jesus asked Peter if he loved Him. When Peter an-swered, "Yes, Lord, you know that I love you," Jesus gave him a chance to prove it by issuing a command, "Take care of my sheep" (John 21:16). If you're continually obey-

[1]Dr. Paul G. Trulin, *Resurrection Life* (Sacramento, Calif.: Harvesters Missionary Society, 1984), p. 150.

ing Jesus, you'll receive His love and the "I love you's" will be spontaneous expressions of your true feelings.

John 14:23 explains how the love of God is put into working order: "Jesus replied, 'If anyone loves me, he will obey my teaching. My father will love him, and we will come to him and make our home with him.' "

It's all action—God shows His love to you in rays of sunshine and fuzzy kittens, but most of all in allowing Jesus to take the punishment that you deserve because of your sin. You respond by accepting this free gift of salvation and obeying His commandments. God comes back by putting His Spirit within you to give you love and joy and power as you obey, and you reply by carrying out His wishes. In response He sends you His blessings.

This love cycle is very satisfying. Christ living in you and you in Him involves a relationship deeper than any expression of human love. It produces a continuous action of loving and being loved. When you give yourself to Jesus with total abandon, you just want to obey more and more commands, because giving and receiving of love is exciting and fulfilling.

There's nothing quite like putting "I love you" into practice.

MEMORIZE

"Whoever has my commands and obeys them, he is the one who loves me. He who loves me will be loved by my Father, and I too will love him and show myself to him" (John 14:21).

VISUALIZE

PERSONALIZE

If I search out all the commands of Jesus and obey them, I'm showing Him that I love Him. If I embrace some doctrine that ignores Jesus, I can't experience God's love. In response to my obedience, Jesus shows His love to me and reveals more and more of himself.

PRAY THE VERSE, APPLYING IT TO YOUR LIFE

Dear God, I will obey every command in your Word, even _____ (something hard for you) to show Jesus that I love Him. I receive your love and know that I will experience more of Jesus' love and become intimately acquainted with Him as I continue to obey.

PUT "I LOVE YOU" INTO PRACTICE

Ask Jesus what specific thing you can do to honor your father and your mother. Ask Jesus how you can help "preach the good news to all creation." Let Him show you what "submit . . . to the governing authorities" means for you. Offer these acts of obedience as sacrifices of love to Jesus and receive His love in return.

The House for Sale on Devil's Drive

Andre was an orphan who lived in the streets of New York City. He had learned to be tough and to steal his way through life.

One day as he was going through a garbage can, a gray-haired man came up to him. Because Andre had heard horrible things about a man who fit his description, terror gripped him. The man, who called himself Mr. Carter, surprised Andre by suggesting, "Son, why don't you come live at my house? I'd like to give you a good home."

Andre was certain that it was the trick of a kidnapper or a murderer. He started to leave.

But Mr. Carter was reassuring, "If you're afraid, I'll just bring your chicken dinner out here." And he did.

Having broken down Andre's fear by consistent kindness, Mr. Carter again extended his invitation to the boy. This time it was accepted.

Andre experienced a lot of love and acceptance and, for the first time in his life, ate three good meals every day and slept in a clean bed.

Once, the longing for the excitement of street-fighting became so strong that he went back to his gang. Certain that Mr. Carter now hated him, he became afraid to go back. However, Mr. Carter went looking for him and showed him compassion and forgiveness. Then Andre stole Mr. Carter's gold watch and sold it on the street to buy some drugs. In spite of all the love demonstrated so consistently, Andre decided that Mr. Carter didn't really love him and never wanted to see him again.

It's pretty easy to see that the "nobody-loves-me" syndrome which Andre is suffering is his own fault. However, you might have an undiagnosed case of it yourself. There's a cure. Jesus prayed to His Father: "I have made you known to them, and will continue to make you known in order that the love you have for me may be in them and that I myself may be in them" (John 17:26). If you really get to know God, you'll find love because God is love.

It's little wonder that so much of the devil's big lie campaign centers on trying to make young people feel that God doesn't want them to have any fun, that God won't forgive and that He is strict and mean and stingy. Don't be deceived by the devil. *The Truth Is That God Is Love and the Better You Get to Know God the More You'll Experience True Love.*

Spend so much time with God and His Word that when the devil whispers, "God won't forgive you," you won't even give it a second thought. Receive so much love from Jesus that you run into His arms when you mess things up instead of thinking that He must hate you for failing. Let His love fill that gnawing emptiness deep down inside. God's love is always there. God is love. It's just that *you* take trips to "Nobody-Loves-Me-Land," or decide to sell your house on Reality Road and buy the one for sale on Devil's Drive.

MEMORIZE

"As the Father has loved me, so have I loved you. Now remain in my love. If you obey my commands, you will remain in my love" (John 15:9–10).

VISUALIZE

PERSONALIZE

Jesus loves me just as much as His father loves Him—and that's an awful lot. I must stick with the fact that He loves me and receive His love. As I get to know Him so well that I trust Him and want to obey Him, I'll always sense His love. My guilt hides His love when I disobey.

PRAY THE VERSE, APPLYING IT TO YOUR LIFE

Dear God, thank you that Jesus loves me with your love. I reject _____ (feeling that God doesn't really love you for one reason or another). Help me to obey your commands. (Confess any sin right now and get back on track.) Keep me from listening to any lie that prevents me from accepting your constant love.

MEDITATE ON SCRIPTURE

Take a card like this with you today. Think about this verse whenever you don't have to concentrate on what you're doing. Let God apply it to your life. As you go to sleep, repeat the verse over and over.

Loving Enemies and Other Difficult People

Her parents were transients who moved into the dilapidated house at the end of the block. Griselda showed up at school dressed in clothes from the last decade. She didn't even bring a notebook. She never smiled or said "hi" to anyone. She seemed suspicious of everyone and always on her guard.

After four months at Roosevelt High, Griselda Graves didn't even have one friend. Melody began to pray for her. Praying for Griselda and opening up to receive more and more of God's love herself, Melody really wanted to express her concern. She gave Griselda some of her own clothes and invited her over for dinner. Griselda began to open up and share some of her problems.

But when Griselda asked if she could borrow twenty dollars, there was something inside Melody that told her this wasn't wise. However, Melody pushed it aside and said, "Of course I'll give money to someone I love."

Soon Melody noticed that Griselda had no intention of paying it back—but she got enough love from Jesus to forgive her friend completely.

A few days later, Griselda told her that she had forgotten to bring her pen to school. "Oh, that's no problem," assured Melody, "I've got an extra in my locker. I'll go get it for you."

"You don't have to bother," replied Griselda. "Just

give me your locker com and I'll get it myself."

Again, Melody felt something down inside trying to stop her, but she thought, "You've got to trust the person you love." And she responded, "68–14–25."

Gradually she realized that Griselda was becoming more and more distant. She knew something was wrong. A week later, she realized that Griselda had stolen her purse out of her locker, and that she now had the keys to her house and her mother's car!

How would she handle this situation? Melody was really discouraged. This had been her first attempt at receiving Jesus' love for a really difficult person. And Jesus really *had* given her love for Griselda. Why did it have to end up like this? Melody just couldn't understand it. Has anyone ever taken advantage of your love? The solution is not to stop loving. It's learning how to love with Jesus' love.

Phil. 1:9–10 gives us the key to this kind of love: "And this is my prayer: that your love may abound more and more in knowledge and depth of insight, so that you may be able to discern what is best." Jesus has two gifts to give you: His love and His wisdom. You need them both if you are to love another person.

If the love you give away comes from what is stored up inside, you'll soon burn out. If you give from a limited supply, you'll grow to resent the "love leeches" that congregate around you. You must consciously reach out to God to receive more of His love many times each day. Then you'll find that He showers you with so much understanding and mercy and affection that it just overflows.

And there'll even be enough left over for enemies and difficult people.

But you also need His wisdom to discern what is best. Loving without seeking God's good judgment results in tremendous complications. After receiving *God's* love for a person, you must earnestly pray for wisdom. Sometimes love must be tough, sometimes cautious, and sometimes demonstrative. But only God can show you what is right for each situation.

The love you get from God is the medicine that can cure the lonely and troubled people you meet. It's just that the wrong dosage given in the wrong way could make things worse instead of better. Daring to love is exciting— and dangerous. Loving with your human love and forgetting to ask God for wisdom can devastate both you and the person you're trying to help. But if you use God's love *and* His wisdom, God will reach out to His world through you.

MEMORIZE

"For this very reason, make every effort to add to your faith goodness; and to goodness, knowledge; and to knowledge, self-control; and to self-control, perseverance; and to perseverance, godliness; and to godliness, brotherly kindness; and to brotherly kindness, love" (2 Pet. 1:5–7).

VISUALIZE

PERSONALIZE

I will remember that love which comes from God rests on a foundation built from faith, goodness, knowledge, self-control, perseverance, godliness, and brotherly kindness. If "love" contradicts one of these qualities, it is not really love.

PRAY THE VERSE, APPLYING IT TO YOUR LIFE

Show me how to deepen my faith and how to put goodness, knowledge, self-control, perseverance, godliness, brotherly kindness and love into my life. Put me back on track if I ever think "love" must exclude one of these virtues.

CHECK YOUR LOVE BY GOD'S STANDARDS

Choose three people: the person whose company you enjoy most, the person you find hardest to love, and one other. Ask God to show you if faith, goodness, knowledge, self-control, perseverance, godliness, and brotherly kindness are the foundations on which this love is built. If not, ask God how you change.

WEEK 13
DAY 4

Join the Exterminators!

It was the first day of school, and Lizette received her schedule during homeroom. Apprehensively, she checked the names of her teachers. Sure enough, there it was—third-hour science with Mr. Gerald Crabtree!

Nearly ready to retire, Mr. Crabtree had become a living legend—the toughest, meanest teacher in the whole district. In fact, Lizette's uncle had flunked his science course and, on occasion, still recounted science room horror stories.

At 10:05 Lizette headed for room 205, commonly referred to as "Jerry's Jail." Lizette trembled a little as she looked at the seating chart on the blackboard and found her chair. Mr. Crabtree's beginning-of-the-year speech fulfilled all her expectations. The kids called this heavy-set bald man "Mussolini" behind his back. Lizette could understand why.

Soon Lizette dreaded third hour and felt that Mr. Crabtree had singled her out as the object of his anger. Even in her dreams she could hear, "Why don't you speak up so everyone can hear?" And one day when she burst into tears, he ridiculed her in front of the class. Although Lizette believed that God answers prayer, she had a very hard time receiving faith for the situation in science class.

One evening as she was reading 1 John, five words caught her eye: "Perfect love drives out fear." She realized that her problem in science class stemmed from fear. She was always afraid of what would happen next. But she couldn't even imagine loving Mr. Crabtree and she didn't even know what perfect love was.

As she prayed for wisdom, she realized that the only love that was perfect was God's love and that she was to love Mr. Crabtree with love she got from God. Remembering that he had lost his wife in a car accident, Lizette prayed that God would help Mr. Crabtree. Now she asked the Lord to show her how to do something special for him.

The first thing God showed her was that she should pray for him daily, and come to his class with a smile. As God put His love in her heart for her science teacher, the fear began to leave.

When they made apple pies in home economics, Lizette gave hers to Mr. Crabtree. He thanked her so much she was embarrassed.

She kept asking God for more love and there was less and less fear. When Mr. Crabtree read the riot act, she'd ask God to give her love for him—and it kept the fear away. Even when he criticized her report in front of the whole class, she didn't fall apart. (She'd stored up some extra love just for the occasion.)

Fear is the symptom that tells you there is lack of love. The Bible teaches that love and fear are opposites; the two can't exist side by side. Keep receiving God's never-ending supply of love, and join the exterminators who do away with fear and doubt.

MEMORIZE

"There is no fear in love. But perfect love drives out fear, because fear has to do with punishment. The man who fears is not made perfect in love" (1 John 4:18).

VISUALIZE

PERSONALIZE

I know that real love has no fear connected with it, because God's perfect love gets rid of the fear of what will happen to me. Fears I have indicate to me that I'm not made perfect in love.

PRAY THE VERSE, APPLYING IT TO YOUR LIFE

Dear Lord, thank you that your life eliminates fear. If I love you, I'll keep your commandments and will have no fear of punishment. The fact that I fear _____ and _____ indicate that I'm not made perfect in love. Lord, perfect your love in me.

LET LOVE DO THE JOB

Make a list of your fears. Write next to each one, "Perfect love drives out fear," then ask God for enough love to drive the fear away.

WEEK 13
DAY 5

Self-Examination

1. Do you have time to fall in love with Jesus? _____
   Do you enjoy His presence every day? _____
   If the answer is no, what are you going to do about it?
   _____
   _____

2. What is *not* true of God's love?
   _____ a. God loves me even when I sin.
   _____ b. God loves me so much He'll never discipline me.
   _____ c. God's love is forever.
   _____ d. There is no place I can hide from God's love.

3. Describe the "love cycle." _____
   _____
   _____

4. What has always been a main topic in the devil's "big lie" campaign?
   _____ a. Eat an apple just like Eve.
   _____ b. Smiling is bad for your health.
   _____ c. God doesn't really love you and He's mean, cruel and stingy.
   _____ d. Taking drugs increases your efficiency.

5. List the things that form the foundation on which love

is built: _____

6. What's the opposite of love?
   ____ a. Hate.
   ____ b. Disgust.
   ____ c. Friction.
   ____ d. Fear.

7. How do I prove to God that I love Him? _____

8. If someone completely takes advantage of your love, what's the problem? _____

9. What verse are you going to internalize to become a stronger Christian?
   ____ a. Neh. 8:10.
   ____ b. 1 Cor. 16:13.
   ____ c. Eph. 6:10.
   ____ d. Other (specify) _____ .

   (Make a card with this verse and start memorizing it right now.)

10. Are you living close enough to Jesus to be a Son reflector? _____
    Where do you need to shape up? _____

---

1. Personal 2. b. 3. I respond to the love God showed in sending Jesus to die for me by accepting His salvation and obeying His commands. He sends His Spirit to live inside me to give me joy and peace and power as I continue to obey and receive more blessings. 4. c. 5. Faith, goodness, knowledge, self-control, perseverance, godliness, brotherly love. 6. d. 7. I keep His commands. 8. It was given without knowledge, or in the wrong way. 9.—10. Personal.